BP
565
.R7

Presented by
The Theosophical Book Gift Institute
Wheaton, Illinois 60187

# ELEMENTARY
# THEOSOPHY

*By*
L. W. ROGERS

Published under a grant from the Kern Foundation

KIRTLEY LIBRARY
COLUMBIA COLLEGE
COLUMBIA, MO 65216

THE THEOSOPHICAL PUBLISHING HOUSE
Wheaton, Ill., U.S.A.
Madras, India / London, England

Copyright 1929
*by*
L. W. Rogers

Seventh Edition
1968

# PREFACE

This book is written for those who are seeking an explanation of life and its purpose—those who are trying to fathom the mystery of the "whence" and the "whither" of the human race. It is not a book of abstractions for the metaphysician. It is for the reader who is in quest of a solution of the mysteries of existence that is devoid of all technical terms and puzzling phrases.

The purpose is to make a very simple presentation of elementary Theosophy. It is certainly elementary throughout but, of course, the ground is not fully covered. The subject is too vast for that. Instead of attempting a complete and detailed exposition of elementary Theosophy, the plan has been rather to discuss its fundamental principles from the viewpoint of "the man in the street."

The fear of death and the hope of immortality are almost universal. Those who are dissatisfied with the old answers to the riddles of life and death, and who insist that faith shall be justified by reason, will find in Theosophy explanations of the puzzling things in life that disregard neither the intuitions of religion nor the facts of science.

Perhaps it is because our modern civilization is so engrossed with material things that we have done so little toward finding a satisfactory philosophy of life. At any rate, we have thoughtlessly accepted much theological absurdity from the Middle Ages. The utter failure to improve very much upon the religious thought of earlier periods is one of the really astounding things of our times. We have traveled fast and gone far in material life, but we have scarcely moved at all in things spiritual. We have worked wonders in invention, we have wrought miracles in science; but we have done little indeed on the ethical side of life.

We need a philosophy of life that is as scientific as it is beautiful, as logical as it is reverent. We need not only sciences material but a science of things spiritual that attacks both ignorance and superstition, with all their paralyzing doubts and their monstrous fears—a science of the soul that satisfies the heart while it proves to the intellect that man is the deathless son of God, and that by right divine he walks the upward way of eternal life.

# CONTENTS

| | | | |
|---|---|---|---|
| Chapter | I. | Theosophy | 7 |
| Chapter | II. | The Immanence of God | 13 |
| Chapter | III. | The Evolution of the Soul | 29 |
| Chapter | IV. | The Continuity of Consciousness | 33 |
| Chapter | V. | The Evolutionary Field | 51 |
| Chapter | VI. | The Mechanism of Consciousness | 59 |
| Chapter | VII. | Death | 71 |
| Chapter | VIII. | The Astral Life | 79 |
| Chapter | IX. | Rebirth: Its Reasonableness | 113 |
| Chapter | X. | Rebirth: Its Justice | 145 |
| Chapter | XI. | Rebirth: Its Necessity | 165 |
| Chapter | XII. | Why We Do Not Remember | 185 |
| Chapter | XIII. | Vicarious Atonement | 201 |
| Chapter | XIV. | The Forces We Generate | 207 |
| Chapter | XV. | Superphysical Evolution | 241 |

# CHAPTER I.

## THEOSOPHY

Rediscovery is one of the methods of progress. Very much that we believe to be original with us at the time of its discovery or invention proves in time to have been known to earlier civilizations. The elevator, or lift, is a very modern invention and we had supposed it to be a natural development of our mechanistic civilization until an antiquarian startled us with the announcement that it was used in Rome over two thousand years ago; not, of course, as we use it, but for the same purpose, and involving the same principles. In the middle of the 19th century our scientific men were enthusiastic over the truths of evolution that were being discovered and placed before western civilization; but as we learn more and more of the thought and intellectual life of the Orient it becomes clear that the idea of evolution was common in that part of the world centuries ago. Even the most recent and startling scientific discoveries occasionally serve to prove that what we had supposed to be the fantastic beliefs of the ancients were really truths of nature that we had not yet discovered. The transmutation of metals is an example. We have already gone far enough in that direction to show that the alchemists of old were not the foolish and superstitious people we had supposed them to be. We have given far too little credit to past civilizations for their achievements and we are coming slowly to understand that we have misjudged them. Our humility must necessarily increase as it becomes clearer that much of our supposed contribution to the world's progress is not invention but rediscovery. We are beginning to see that it is not safe to put aside without careful examination an idea or a belief that was current in the world thousands of years ago. Like the supposed folly of the alchemists it may contain profound truths of nature that have thus far been foreign to our modes of thinking.

Theosophy is both very old and very new—very old because its truths were known and taught in the oldest civilizations, and very new because it includes the latest investigations of the present day. It is sometimes said by those who desire to speak lightly of it that it is a philosophy borrowed from the Buddhists, or at least from the Orient. That is, of course, an erroneous view. It is true that the Buddhists hold some beliefs in common with Theosophists. It is also true that Methodists hold some beliefs in common with Unitarians, but that does not show that Unitarianism was borrowed from Wesley! Buddhism is not unique in resembling Theosophy. In the same list may be placed the Vedanta philosophy, the Cabala of the Jews, the teachings of the Christian Gnostics and the philosophy of the Stoics. None of them is Theosophy, but in their treatment of various truths of nature all of them are, at one point or another, in agreement with Theosophy; and this sometimes leads to the hasty conclusion that they are identical with it.

The more general charge must also be denied; Theosophy is not something transplanted from the Orient. As it is taught today in Europe and America it is probably unknown to the masses of the Orient, for the great general truths it embodies have here the special application and peculiar emphasis required by a very different civilization; but that theosophical principles were earlier known and were more widely accepted in the Orient is quite true. That fact can in no way lessen their value to us. Precisely the same thing is true of mathematics. Mathematical science reached European civilization directly from the Arabs, but we do not foolishly decline to make use of the knowledge on that account.

The literal meaning of the word Theosophy is self-evident—knowledge of God. It has three aspects, determined by the different ways in which the human being acquires knowledge—through the study of concrete facts, by the study of the relationship of the individual consciousness to its source, and through the use of reasoning faculties in constructing a logical explanation of life and its purpose. In one aspect it is, therefore, a science: it deals with the tangible, with the facts and phenomena of the material scientist and makes its appeal through the evidence of the physical senses. In another aspect it is a religion: it deals with the relationship between the source of all consciousness and its multiplicity of individual expressions; with the complex relationships that arise between these personalities;

with the duties and obligations which thus come into existence; with the evolution of the individual consciousness and its ultimate translation to higher spheres. In its other aspect it is a philosophy of life: it deals with man, his origin, his evolution, his destiny; it seeks to explain the universe and to throw a flood of light upon the problem of existence that will enable those who study its wisdom to go forward in their evolution rapidly, safely and comfortably, instead of blundering onward in the darkness of ignorance, reaping as they go the painful harvests of misdirected energy.

While Theosophy is a science and a philosophy it is not, in the same full sense, a religion. It has its distinctively religious aspect, it is true, but when we speak of a religion we usually have in mind a certain set of religious dogmas and a church that propagates them. Theosophy has neither. Theosophy is a universal thing like mathematics—a body of natural truths applicable to all phases of life. It sees all religions as equally important, as peculiarly adapted to the varying civilizations in which they are found, and it presents a synthesis of the fundamental principles upon which all of them rest.

From all of this it will be seen that there is a vast difference between Theosophy and theology. Theosophy declares the immortality of man but not as a religious belief. It appeals to the scientific facts in relation to the nature of consciousness. It knows no such word as "faith," as it is ordinarily used. Its faith arises from the constancy of natural law, the balance and sanity of nature. Theosophy is very old in that it is the great fund of ancient wisdom about man and his earth, that has come down through countless centuries, reaching far back into prehistoric times. Added to that hoary wisdom are the up-to-date facts that have been acquired by its most successful students, who have evolved their consciousness to levels transcending the physical senses—facts which, however, do not derive their authority from the method of their discovery but from their inherent reasonableness. A detailed discussion of such methods of consciousness and the proper value to be placed upon such investigations rightly belongs to another chapter. It is enough now to warn the reader against the error of confusing the pronouncements of pseudo-psychism with the work of the psychic scientists who have already done much toward placing a scientific foundation beneath the hope of immortality.

## CHAPTER II.

## THE IMMANENCE OF GOD

All the differences of opinion about immortality run back to the various conceptions which people hold of the universe. The materialist's belief that consciousness ceases when the body dies arises from his conception of a universe in which consciousness is produced by the evolution of forms. He begins his universe with the declaration that matter and energy exist; that they have always existed; that they give rise to forms and intelligence; and that, therefore, when the forms disintegrate the intelligence they expressed ceases to be. The materialist usually makes a strong point of the scientific aspect of his philosophy and frequently reminds us that the belief in immortality is merely a hope with no substantial basis—a sort of delusion possible only to those who cannot reason soundly.

The Theosophist begins with the declaration that God exists; that He is eternal; that matter and energy are emanations from Him; that all degrees of intelligence are expressions of His life. In what way is the materialist's hypothesis more scientific or reasonable than the Theosophist's? Both start with a first cause and postulate an eternal universe. The difference between them is that the Theosophist postulates an *intelligent* first cause. Is it not just as reasonable to say that mind has always existed as to say that matter has always existed? Nobody will deny that consciousness is higher than matter. With one or the other, or with both, we must begin. Why begin with the lower? In asserting that consciousness has always existed, what rule of logic do we violate that the materialist does not violate with the declaration that matter has always existed? We know that consciousness can and does create forms from matter. Every building is visible evidence of that fact. Is it not, then, more logical to think that eternal consciousness has fashioned the forms that fill the world than to believe that eternal matter has created man?

Those of us who believe in an intelligent first cause are sometimes reminded of the child who, when told that God had made the earth, asked his mother who made God; and thoughtless people triumphantly remind us that the question is unanswerable. But precisely the same trouble arises if you ask how matter first came to exist. It is just as hard to account for the materialist's original matter as to account for the Theosophist's original consciousness. The finite mind cannot comprehend eternity. It is difficult to see how there was never a beginning, yet it is quite impossible to think of an end; for the mind at once asks, "What after that?" Tennyson put well that limitation of the finite mind when he wrote, "It is hard to believe in God; it is harder not to believe in Him." In these basic declarations, then, with which each begins the universe, the Theosophist cannot be said to be either illogical or unscientific be-

## The Immanence of God

cause he starts with the higher factor instead of with the lower—with eternal consciousness instead of with eternal matter and force.

Next comes the task, for each, of showing that his hypothesis satisfactorily explains the universe as it now stands. Think for a moment of what the materialist must do! He must show that from a universe of original chaos, the reign of law springs up; that from unguided matter has arisen the human race with its wondrous expressions of genius and its marvelous achievements in science; that with no original intelligence nature has produced an intelligence that is steadily rising to colossal heights; that from no morality has come a morality so sublime that men sacrifice their lives for the common good; that all the exalted emotions of the race have no higher source than the mud beneath our feet; that from senseless dust has come the jester's wit; the inventor's craft, the artist's dream, the sage's mind, the martyr's zeal, the mother's love, and all the subtle lights and shades and heights and depths within the heart and brain of man! It is only necessary to state the case in order to see its absurdity. The materialist often refers to the tendency of one class of his opponents to put aside natural law and reason and rely upon faith and miracle; but if ever there was an appeal to the miraculous it is found in the belief that matter, the slave, created mind, the master!

There is more wrong with the materialist's philosophy than his acceptance of a hypothesis that is so inadequate, and the more science learns about nature the worse does his case become. Matter is the great fetish in his system of things. Deprive him of his hypothesis of eternal matter and the foundation of his philosophy is gone; yet that is precisely what modern science in recent years has done. By a single discovery it has exploded all the old theories and shown that the supposed ultimate atom is a composite thing. In other words, matter as known to the physical senses is just as much an illusion as the apparent movement of the sun through the sky. Matter is in reality one form or phase of energy, and if we put the scientific dictum in ordinary words it comes substantially to this: that matter is the lowest expression of life. Where, then, does the materialist stand? Under the searchlight of modern science his eternal matter is seen to be eternal life. No wonder so great a scientist as Sir Oliver Lodge wrote in one of his books that it may well be doubted if there is any longer such a thing in the world as scientific materialism. There is unquestionably widespread materialism but it is not up-to-date with science. It is merely repeating as facts theories that are exploded.

Let us amplify the hypothesis that God eternally exists, and that the material world is but an emanation from Him. If it will help those who think in materialistic terms to use language that is not intimately associated with religion, we can say that a first cause eternally exists and that its characteristics are wisdom, power and compassion. That comes to the same thing as saying that God is good, wise and powerful. The Theosophists regard that first cause as an inconceivably mighty spiritual entity, of wisdom, love and power, but he does not, by any means, hold the anthropomorphic conception of the Supreme Being so popular with millions of people. The declaration that the solar system is an emanation from God is to be taken in the most literal sense. Now that we have reached the point in scientific knowledge where matter is seen to be a form of energy, it is not so difficult to understand the old doctrine of the immanence of God. If one thinks of our solar system in its primordial condition it will be still easier to see it as the emanation of a central Being— as mighty streams of energy flowing outward from Him and gradually differentiating into various classes of matter. The theosophical view is that all forces are His forces. Consequently there is no such thing as an unintelligent force. It may, like the force we call gravity, be absolutely impersonal, but it is not unintelligent. It has its purpose in a mighty plan. All energy, all matter, all life in the system, are His life. The consciousness of an insect and that of man are but the varying expressions of the one eternal life that we call God. That is the old doctrine of immanence—that His life thrills through every form and every atom of the universe, that His consciousness embraces it all, that His will sustains it all. There is nothing in the universe that is not some kind of expression of His life. It may be at the human, at the animal, at the vegetable, or only at the mineral level of evolution, but it is none the less an expression of the life of the Supreme Being. The consciousness in man is of a high order and we call it self-consciousness. The consciousness in matter we name chemical affinity; but the two differ only in degree.

There again science has rendered great service by showing that the life in a mineral responds to stimuli and can even be poisoned, as certainly as an animal can. The scientific discovery that swept away the theory of the ultimate atom, and showed that it is in fact but a center of force, is the most stupendous revelation of modern life. It is still too new to have registered its full significance in the consciousness of the race. Like all revolutions it will be followed by slow readjustment of thought; but when that readjustment is complete, there will no longer be difficulty in seeing that matter is but a form of life, and that all life is one life.

Why then, it may be asked, is that one life more intelligent at some levels than at others? Because at low levels it is being only very partially expressed through dense encasements of matter, while at higher levels it is being more fully expressed. Or, we may say that at low levels life is in the kindergarten learning response to simple vibrations, while at high levels it is at the university getting lessons that can be learned only from complex vibrations; but all life is some phase of God's life, for nothing in our solar system exists outside the Supreme Being.

Some devout people seem to think of God as a manufacturer and of heaven as a soul factory! To them God and the human soul are as separate as a teacher and his pupils; but if they will carefully read their Scriptures they will find there the most explicit statements to the contrary. It is not said that by His power and permission we exist. It does not say that near Him we live, but it says very pointedly

## THE IMMANENCE OF GOD 19

that *in* Him we live, we move, we have our being.

How can that be? How can one being exist literally within another? It is simplicity itself when we think of the solar system as an emanation of the Supreme Being, as something generated from a central life, as an expression of that life which gives rise to the two poles within it that we know as consciousness and matter. The human soul is an individualized fragment of that divine life. Of course our limited consciousness can only imperfectly comprehend it. Imagine that central life of our universe that we call God to be like an eternal light, sending its rays out into space. Imagine those rays, as they are generated and travel outward, having the power to set up within themselves an action that results in differentiation, so that they become at last two distinct types of rays, one corresponding to what we know as life, and the other to what we know as matter. Imagine rotatory currents that imprison the rays of light within the currents of matter. Imagine that the farther the rays get from their source the feebler they become until, at a vast distance, instead of being the blinding light near the central source, they are merely a feeble glow in the void. Then that fragment of a ray, enmeshed in intervening matter but still dimly glowing because it is of the very nature of the central light, of which it is an actual portion, will represent the relationship of the soul to God. It is literally a spark of the divine fire, and latent within it are the characteristics of that central light from which it originated. The theosophical conception of the soul is that it is literally an *emanation* of God, and since it is therefore of His own essence it becomes clear why Theosophists assert that man is a god in the making.

Anybody who analyzes that stupendous truth, and ponders over it, will gradually get a truer understanding of some of the marvelous facts about consciousness which material science cannot explain. He will see that in such astounding phases of human consciousness as premonitions, which sometimes bring into the physical brain knowledge of an impending tragedy, or of a future event, the characteristic of omniscience is no longer puzzling. The soul is of the essential nature of God, who *is* omniscience. At a lower level of evolution than man there is an equally clear explanation of animal instinct. What is it? Physical science has never been able to answer that question. It can only marvel that an unreasoning creature like a bird, or a wild pig, exhibits a wisdom that, within limited scope, is often superior to the talents of man; but the thing ceases to be miraculous when we reckon it from the hypothesis of the immanence of God and remember that we are again dealing with what, in reality, is another phase of the one supreme life.

It is no truer that an acorn is an oak in the making than that man is a god in the making; but the potentialities within the acorn must pass through various stages before the future tree comes into existence. It must lie long in the soil, slowly changing from within, before it can even send out a tiny sprout, which has little likeness to a tree. As with man, the likeness to the cosmic parent is not in outward form but in inward life. Slowly the latent power of the acorn comes into expression. It reaches downward into the soil for anchorage and upward into the air for the true and full expression of its being. There is little semblance between its first sprout and the rugged and powerful tree in its completed growth. Even thus it is in the soul's evolution. It is divine from its inception but its wisdom is undeveloped. Its power is latent. It is only a spark of the divine life that dimly glimmers in its material prison. In the lower kingdoms it very slowly, through long periods of time, lays the foundation for the self-consciousness that will dawn only at the human level. There it reaches individual existence and the divine spark expands into the human soul.

Of course it is not, at that stage of its evolution, the soul as we know it now. It might truly be called the nascent soul. It is only just above the level of the animal kingdom and in the beginning of human development. It differs from the most intelligent animal in that it now has the human mind but it is the mind of the infant soul of savage man. It can use fire and construct a shelter but a long period of evolution must pass before it enters the stage of civilized life. In that evolution life and the form are developing together. The savage is the savage only because his latent mental and moral qualities are unevolved. Precisely the same spark of the life of God is in him, and constitutes his inmost being, but only long experience in the material world can stimulate and arouse it into action and finally raise him to the level of civilized man.

The antagonism between scientific and religious thought was the cause of the greatest controversy that occurred in the intellectual world in the nineteenth century. If the early teaching of the Christian Church had not been lost the conflict could not have arisen. The Gnostic philosophers, who were the intellect and heart of the church, had a knowledge of nature so true that it could not possibly come into collision with any fact of science; but unfortunately they were enormously outnumbered by the ignorant, and the authority passed wholly into the hands of the latter. It was inevitable that misunderstanding should follow. The gross materialization of the early teaching, the superstition, the bigotry and the persecution of the Middle Ages was a perfectly natural result. That perverted, materialistic view has come down to us, and even now gives trend to the religious thought of Western civilization. Of that degradation of the early teaching the Encyclopedia Britannica says:

> The conception of God as wholly external to man, a purely mechanical theory of creation, is throughout Christendom regarded as false to the teaching of the New Testament as also to Christian experience.

It is, indeed, false to the teaching of the Christ but if it is so regarded "throughout Christendom" it is only on the part of its scholars; most certainly not by the masses of the people. The popular conconception is undeniably that the relationship between God and man is identical with that between an inventor and his machine. It is an absolutely anthropomorphic view of the Supreme Being and thinks of God as being apart from man in precisely the same sense that a father is apart from his son. It may be an exalted, idealized conception of the relationship of father and son but it is nevertheless just that relationship, and along that line runs nearly all the teaching and preaching of those who speak officially in modern religious interpretation. Emerson sought to counteract that popular misconception but he was regarded as a heretic by all but an infinitesimal portion of the church of his time.

The idea of the immanence of God is as different from the popular conception as noontide is different from midnight. It is so radically different that one who accepts that ancient belief must put aside his old ideas of what man is and raise him in dignity and potential power to a level that will, at first, seem actually startling; for it means, in its uttermost significance, that God and man are but two phases of the one eternal life and consciousness that constitute our universe! The idea of the immanence of God is that He *is* the universe; although He is also more than it is; that the solar system is an emanation of the Supreme Being as clouds are an emanation of the sea. This conception makes a man a *part* of God, having potentially within him all the attributes and powers of the Supreme Being. It is the idea that nothing exists except God and that humanity is one portion of Him—one phase of His being. The immanence of God is a conception of the universe that puts science and religion in harmony with each other, because miraculous creation disappears and evolutionary creation takes its place.

Although the mechanical conception of the universe has such widespread dominion in Occidental thought, the immanence of God is plainly taught and repeatedly emphasized in the Christian scriptures. "For in Him we live, and move, and have our being," is certainly very explicit and admits of no anthropomorphic interpretation. It could not be said that a son lives and moves in his father. The declaration presents a closer relationship—the relationship of a lesser consciousness within a greater, *and constituting a part of it.* The essentially divine nature of man is made clear in the declaration in Genesis that he is an image of God. To say that the likeness is on the material side would, of course, be absurd. In divine essence, in latent power, in potential spirituality, man is an image of God, because he is a part of Him. The same idea is more directly put in the Psalms with the assertion, "ye are gods."* If the idea of the immanence of God is sound then man, as a literal fragment of the consciousness of the Supreme Being, is an embryo god, destined to ultimately evolve his latent powers into perfect expression.

The oneness of life was explicitly asserted by Jesus. Emerson's teaching of the immanence of God is unmistakable in both his prose and poetry. "There is no bar or wall," he says, "in the soul where man, the effect, ceases and God, the Cause, begins." Still more explicitly he puts it:

---

* Psalms LXXXII—6.

The realms of being to no other bow;
Not only all are Thine, but all art Thou.

The statement is as complete as it is emphatic. "Not only all are Thine, *but all are Thou.*" It is an unqualified assertion that humanity is a part of God, as leaves are a part of a tree—not something a tree has created in the sense that a man creates a machine but something that is an emanation of the tree, and is a living part of it. Thus only has God made man. Humanity is a growth, a development, an emanation, an evolutionary expression of the Supreme Being.

It is upon the unity of all life that Theosophy bases its declaration of universal brotherhood, regarding it as a fact in nature. The theosophical conception is that men are separated in form but are united in the one consciousness which is the life base of the universe. Their relationship to each other is somewhat like that of the fingers to each other—they are separate individuals on the form side but they are united in the one consciousness that animates the hand. If we imagine each finger to possess a consciousness of its own, which is limited to itself and cannot pass beyond to the hand, we shall have a fair analogy of the unity and identity of interests of all living things. Under such circumstances an injury to one finger would not appear to the others as an injury to them, but if the finger consciousness could be extended to the hand the reality of the injury to all would be apparent. Likewise an injury to any human being is literally an injury to the race. The race does not recognize the truth of it because, and only because, of the limitation of consciousness. Lowell put the fact clearly when he wrote:

> He's true to God who's true to man.
> Wherever wrong is done
> To the humblest and weakest
> 'Neath the all-beholding sun,
> That wrong is also done to us;
> And they are slaves most base
> Whose love of right is for themselves,
> And not for all the race.

"He's true to God who's true to man" because they are one life; because they are but different expressions of the one eternal consciousness; because they are as inseparable as the light and the warmth of the sun. It follows that being true to man is fidelity to God.

The popular idea is that people should be moral because that sort of conduct is pleasing to the Supreme Being and that He will, in the life beyond physical existence, in some way punish those who have broken the moral laws. It is belief in an external authority that threatens punishment as a deterrent to law breaking, as a state devises penalties commensurate with offences, while the immanence of God represents a condition in which not punishments, but consequences, automatically follow all violations of natural law. Under such a state of affairs it requires no penalties, but only knowledge, to insure right conduct, for there is no possible escape from the consequences of an evil act.

It is not difficult to see the relative value of the two systems of thought when put to a practical test in human affairs. Imagine an unscrupulous man of great mental capacity who is amassing an enormous fortune through sharp practices that enable him to acquire the earnings of others while he safely keeps just within the law. We can point out to him that while he is not violating the law, and cannot therefore be prosecuted, he is nevertheless inflicting injury upon others and consequently public opinion will condemn him. Such a man usually cares nothing at all for public opinion and he sees no good reason why he should not continue in his injurious work; but if he can be made to see that all life is one and that we are so knit together in consciousness that an injury to another must ultimately react upon the person who inflicts it; if he once clearly understands that to enslave another is to put chains upon himself, that to maim another is to maim himself, he will require neither the fear of an exterior hell nor the threat of legal penalties to induce him to follow a moral course. He would see that his own larger and true self-interest could be served only when his conduct was in harmony with the welfare of all. It is but a simple statement of the truth to say that the immanence of God, when fully understood, furnishes a scientific basis of morality.

## CHAPTER III.

## THE EVOLUTION OF THE SOUL

If we accept the idea of the immanence of God we shall be forced to abandon belief in a miraculous instantaneous creation of man, and of the earth on which he exists. The absurd, unscientific idea that the race came from an original human pair must be replaced by the hypothesis of the evolutionary creation of the soul by God.

It was about the fact of evolution that the great storm of controversy raged between scientists and theologians in the middle of the nineteenth century, and later. The evolutionary truths were not at first well understood. They seemed to question or deny the existence of God. Deep within humanity is intuitive religious belief. It is a natural faith that transcends all facts, like the faith of a child in its mother. Because evolution was contrary to all preconceived ideas of the earth's inception it seemed at first to shatter faith and destroy hope, and against fact and reason itself rose the protest of intuition with spiritual intensity. People felt more than they reasoned, and cried out that science was about to destroy the belief in God; but time has proved that they had merely misinterpreted the meaning of evolution. Further understanding has shown that, instead of destroying the belief in a Supreme Being, evolution has given us a new and better understanding of the whole matter and has placed the hope of immortality on firmer ground than it previously occupied.

Evolution is now generally accepted. No broadly educated person thinks of questioning it. That all things in the physical world have become what they are through a long, slow, gradual development and that organisms perfect in form and complex in function have evolved from simpler ones is everywhere accepted by scientists. The age of miracle has passed and belief in miracle has also passed so far as its relation to the material world is concerned. It is no longer necessary to have a belief in an anthropomorphic God, performing feats in defiance of natural law, in order to account for that which exists. Science has reduced the cosmos to comprehension and shown that, given nebulous physical matter, we can understand how the earth came into existence.

But why should we stop with the application of the laws of evolution to material things? Only the outright materialist, who asserts that life is a product of matter, can logically do so. Those who accept the idea of the existence of the soul must necessarily accept the idea of the evolution of the soul. How can consciousness possibly escape the laws that evolve the media for the expression of consciousness? There must be the evolution of mind as certainly as there is evolution of matter. The material and the spiritual, form and life, are inseparable. Indeed, scientific progress has now brought us to the point where matter, as such, practically disappears and

## The Evolution of the Soul

we are face to face with the fact that matter is really but a manifestation of energy. How is it longer possible to speak of the soul and not accept the evolution of the soul? Psychology is no less a science than physiology. The phenomena of consciousness are as definitely studied as physical phenomena, and it is no more difficult to account for myriads of souls than to account for millions of suns and their planets. The scientists who have taken the position that the universe has a spiritual side as well as a material side are among the most eminent and distinguished of the modern world. If evolution has produced the starry heavens from the material side it has likewise evolved the human souls of our world, and other worlds, from the spiritual side. It is no more difficult to understand the one than the other.

From the scientific viewpoint the old popular belief in the creation of the earth and the race by an act suddenly accomplished is, of course, preposterous. If we could know nothing back of the present moment and were called upon to account for the world as we see it—with its cities, its ships and railways, its cultivated fields and parks—many people who still believe in the instantaneous creation of the soul would save themselves much mental exertion by declaring that God had made it all as it stands for the use and entertainment of man; yet it would be utterly absurd to think of the world leaping into existence instantaneously—nothing existing one day and all trains running on time between ready-made cities the next, carrying ready-made people about! It sounds ridiculous only because we are putting it in matter-of-fact terms, but in very truth it is less ludicrous than thinking of the instantaneous creation of the creators of cities and railways.

The belief that humanity is a sudden creation is possible because of the very vague ideas of what souls are. The chief difficulty with the popular notion that a human soul is as new as the body it inhabits is that it is an indefinite conception of life, and the moment we begin to think seriously about it the absurdity of the thing becomes apparent. Such an idea has no relationship to the processes of reasoning. How can one reason with a man who believes it possible for a soul to spring into existence from the void? When it settles the whole matter to say, "God did it," why reason about it?

One thing that prevents us from believing, not only that millions of souls were created in the twinkling of an eye, but also that the world as it now is was likewise suddenly created, is that we know quite definitely the natural history of the world a little way into the past, and that history affirms that the earth and all life on it is the product of slow evolutionary growth.

The evolution of the soul places the realm of religion on a scientific basis. Not only the origin of the soul but its development and its destiny at once appear in a new light. The mind is instinctively impressed with the dignity of the idea of the evolution of the soul, which, with its corollary, the immanence of God, makes the divinity of man a fact in nature.

## CHAPTER IV.

## THE CONTINUITY OF CONSCIOUSNESS

One of the really remarkable facts of modern life is the disinclination to accept at apparent value the scientific and other evidence there is to prove that consciousness persists after the death of the physical body. There is in existence a large amount of such evidence and much of it is offered by scientists of the highest standing; yet the average man continues to speak of the subject as though nothing about it had yet been definitely learned. It is the tendency of the human mind to adjust itself very slowly to the facts as they are discovered. Sometimes more than a generation passes away between the discovery and the general acceptance of a great truth. When we recall the intense opposition to the introduction of steam-driven boats and the slowness with which the world settles down to any radical change in its methods of thinking, it will perhaps seem less remarkable that the truth about the life after bodily death has waited so long for general recognition.

The evidence upon which a belief in the continuity of consciousness is based is of two kinds—that furnished by physical science and that furnished by psychic science. Together they make a very complete case.

The printed evidence of the first—physical science—is voluminous. In addition to that gathered by the Society for Psychical Research, monumental in itself, there are the researches and experiments by the scientists of England, France and Italy, among whom are Crookes, Lodge, Flammarion, and many others of almost equal fame. Crookes was a pioneer in the work of studying the human consciousness and tracing its activities beyond the change called death. All of that keenness of intellect and great scientific knowledge which enabled him to make so many valuable discoveries and inventions, and won for him world-wide fame, were brought to bear upon the subject, and for a period of four years he patiently investigated and experimented. Many illustrated articles prepared by him, fully describing his work, were published at the time in *The Quarterly Journal of Science* of which he was then the editor.

Three vital points in psychic research were established by Sir William Crookes. One was that there is psychic force. He demonstrated its existence by levitation. He showed next, that the force is directed by intelligence. By various clever experiments he obtained most conclusive evidence of that fact. He then demonstrated that the intelligence directing the force is not that of living people. Crookes also went exhaustively into the subject of materialization and here, again, he was remarkably successful. He was the first scientist to photograph the materialized human form and to engage in direct conversation with the person who thus returned from the mysterious life beyond. This evidence from the camera must be regarded as particularly interesting. It was received with much amazement at the time, but that was before we had revised our erroneous ideas about the nature of matter and before the day of liquid air. Materialization is no longer a startling idea, for that is precisely what liquid air is—a condensation of invisible matter to the point where it becomes tangible and can be seen, weighed, measured, and otherwise known to the physical senses.

These things Sir William Crookes did upon his own premises and under the most rigid conditions of scientific research. All the methods and mechanism known to modern science were employed and he finally announced his complete satisfaction and his full acceptance of the genuineness of the phenomena observed.

As Sir William Crookes was the earliest, Sir Oliver Lodge was one of the later famous scientists who have taken up the investigation of the continuity of consciousness. In a lecture upon the subject, before the Society for the Advancement of Science, he declared not only that the subject of life after physical death was one which science might legitimately and profitably investigate but that the existence of an invisible realm had been established. He declared that "a new continent" of an intangible world had been discovered, and added, "already a band of daring investigators have landed on its treacherous but promising shores."

Different scientists make a specialty of certain kinds of psychic investigation and while Crookes made a detailed and careful study of materialization,

Lodge gave equally painstaking efforts to investigations by the use of that class of sensitives known as "mediums." A medium is not necessarily clairvoyant, and usually is not. A person in whose body the etheric matter easily separates from the denser matter is a medium and can readily be utilized as a sort of telephone between the visible and the invisible planes. A medium is an abnormal person and is a good medium in proportion to the degree of abnormality. If the etheric matter of the body is easily extruded the physical body readily falls into the trance condition and the mechanism of conversation can be operated by the so-called "dead" person who has temporarily taken possession of it. In such cases it is not the medium who speaks for the "dead" communicator. He is speaking directly himself, but he may often do it with great difficulty and not always succeed in accurately expressing the thought he has in mind. He may have to contend with other thoughts, moods and emotions than his own and to those who understand something of his difficulties it is not strange that such communications are frequently unsatisfactory. It is not often that an analogy can be found that will give a physical plane comprehension of a superphysical condition, but perhaps a slight understanding may be had by thinking of a "party line" telephone that any one of several people may use at any moment that he can succeed in getting possession of it. A listener attempting to communicate with one of them may find that others are constantly "switching in," much to his confusion. If distinction of voices due to sound were eliminated and then a stenographic record were to be made of all words reaching the listener he would find that it would often be fragmentary and trivial. That would not, however, prove that the conversation did not come from living beings nor that there was not at least one intelligent person among them. That scientists engaged in psychic research have similar experiences proves nothing more.

It seems to be a common opinion that the evidential value of such psychic communications, even under the direction of a skillful scientist, cannot be very great; but it is not at all difficult for the investigator to direct his work not only to incidents unknown to the medium, but to scientific facts which the medium cannot possibly comprehend. It is a matter of common knowledge that mediums are usually people without technical scientific knowledge. A few of them have a fair degree of education while many of them are illiterate. Some of the most celebrated belong to the peasant class of Europe.

Let us suppose that an investigating scientist is about to attempt to communicate with a scientist who has passed on to join the living dead. He will ask technical scientific questions that nobody but a scientist can answer and that the medium can not even understand when they are answered. Let us suppose that he gets a communication from the medium's hand signed by a great author. The living dead man writes a criticism, let us say, of some new book and does it in his characteristic style, full of the power of keen analysis and sound literary judgment. Surely nobody can believe that the medium is producing such things on her own account. If she could do so she would not be earning her living as a medium.

The scientists do not stop there. We often hear the expression "cross-correspondence." Just what do they mean by that and in what way does it indicate the personal identity of a dead man who is communicating? The principle may be illustrated by the hotel clerk's method. Sometimes a guest leaves a sum of money with the clerk, and he wishes to be perfectly sure of the guest's identity when he returns to claim it. He requests him to put his signature on a card. Then he tears the card in two, gives him one piece and keeps the other. That gives him a double proof of identity. When the guest comes for his money he must first write his name and then produce the piece of card that fits into the ragged edge of the piece the clerk has retained, the two together making the whole and restoring the signature. It's one of the simplest but most satisfactory proofs possible. Neither piece of that card alone is intelligible. If one piece should be lost and others should find it nobody could read it or make anything of it. Nobody could know the full name unless he had the other fragment. He knows only about the part he holds. He may be a thief and may earnestly desire to use what he has found to defraud, but he is helpless because he has only one of the two parts it requires to make an intelligible whole. That is the principle involved in identity by cross-correspondence. Part of a message is written through one medium and part through another medium at an-

## The Continuity of Consciousness

other time in another place and neither part presents a complete statement or has coherence until it is fitted into the other part; and that prevents a medium who might be dishonest from manufacturing a story that may be more or less plausible.

We are by no means wholly dependent upon scientific investigation for evidence that the dead still live. Hundreds of people are sufficiently sensitive to have some personal knowledge of the matter. The number is far beyond what it appears to be for two reasons. One is that the average person fears ridicule and keeps his own counsel about his occult experiences. The other is the feeling that communications from departed relatives are too sacred and personal for public discussion. Tens of thousands of people have seen demonstrations at spiritualistic seances which, while possessing little evidential value from the scientific viewpoint, nevertheless have a legitimate place in the great mass of psychic phenomena. Still more convincing is the evidence furnished in homes where some member of the family acts as automatic writer or medium.

The most satisfactory evidence is not always scientific evidence. What can be more convincing than the evidence furnished in one's home by members of the family? There is much such evidence, obtained both through mediums and by automatic writing.

Automatic writing—that is, the control of the hand of a living person to record the thoughts of another who has lost the physical body—is perhaps one of the least objectionable ways in which communications have come from the astral world, and to it we are indebted for some useful books with interesting accounts of the life in the unseen regions. Here, of course, as elsewhere, discrimination must be used, for the wise and foolish, the useful and useless are to be found side by side. In accepting or rejecting, one must use his common sense just as he does on this plane in separating the valuable from the worthless. In such matters we should not lose sight of the fact that the living dead are unchanged in intellect and morality. The genius here is the genius there and the living fool is not different from the dead one. It is often those who know the least who are the most anxious to tell it and the medium or automatic writer sometimes gives them the opportunity. Consequently we get many foolish communications and an enormous amount of commonplace platitude is delivered at seances. Nevertheless it is equally true that striking evidence of personal identity is sometimes secured.

There is much valuable non-scientific evidence that the consciousness survives the loss of the physical body and it frequently comes from sources that insure respectful attention. The two following stories of that kind are cited as corroboration of the scientific evidence.

Little touches of the personality often constitute the most convincing of all evidence. It is one thing to show that people in general live after physical death. It is quite a different matter to establish the personal identity of one of them who is communicating, and that is one of the vital points involved. W. J. Stillman, the eminent journalist, gives us in his memoirs some valuable evidence on personal identity. In his earlier years he had studied art in London. Shortly before the death of Turner, the great artist had volunteered to give Stillman some advice on painting, but had not redeemed the promise at the time of passing away. Stillman had a friend whose daughter was mediumistic and he decided to experiment. Immediately on beginning the seance an entity claiming to be Turner took possession of the girl's body. Stillman asked his questions silently, speaking no words, but mentally requesting Turner to write his name. The only reply was an emphatic shake of the head. He then asked if he would give some advice on painting. The response was another decided negative. Stillman felt that he was foolishly wasting his time and declared the seance at an end. The girl sat silent. Then after a moment she slowly arose with the air of decrepitude, took a lithograph from the wall and went through the pantomime of stretching a sheet of paper on a drawing board, sharpening a pencil, tracing the outline, the washing-in of a drawing, etc., and then proceeded to show a simple but surprising method of taking out the lights. "Do you mean to say that Turner got his effects in that way?" asked the incredulous young artist. The answer was an emphatic affirmative. Stillman then asked if the central passage of sunlight and shadow through rain in the well known drawing "Llanthony Abbey" by Turner, had been done in that way and was answered by another emphatic affirmative. So sure was the young artist that this could not be true that he gave it up in disgust and abruptly left. A few weeks later Stillman was calling upon Ruskin and related the experience. Ruskin, who had known the celebrated dead artist intimately, declared that the contrariness of the medium at the beginning of the seance was remarkably characteristic of Turner; but what was much more to the point, in the way of evidence, was that the drawing in question was in Ruskin's possession and eagerly it was brought down from the wall for examination. After close scrutiny the great art critic and the young artist agreed that, beyond dispute, the drawing *had* been done in the way described.

Such evidence has an added value when it comes from those who are neither spiritualists nor professional investigators, but who have the things they doubt thrust upon them in such a convincing manner that they feel impelled to record their experience for the enlightenment of others. In the last literary work[*] done by Carl Schurz, we are given, quite incidentally, his testimony that at a seance soon after the Civil War he was told the future in such detail as to leave no possible room for the usual explanation of coincidence. It was in July, 1865, when Schurz was on his way to Washington, whither he had been summoned by President Johnson, that he stopped in Philadelphia at the home of his friend, Dr. Tiedemann. The doctor's daughter, about fifteen years old, could do automatic writing. As a matter of interest and amusement in the family circle the girl gave an exhibition of her psychic abilities. When

---

[*] *Reminiscences of Carl Schurz*, Vol. III, p. 154.

Schurz was invited to ask for a communication he very naturally requested one from the recently deceased President Lincoln, for he had been personally acquainted with him. The girl wrote a message purporting to come from Lincoln. It related to politics and proved, in time, to have been an accurate prophecy of most unexpected facts which would not transpire for more than three years! Schurz lived in Wisconsin at the time and had no intention of changing his residence, nor did he do so until two years later. The message which the girl wrote asserted that Schurz would be elected to the United States senate *from Missouri*. He did not regard the message as authentic and naturally enough considered the prophecy absurd. In 1867 he took up his residence in St. Louis and in January, 1869, he was elected United States senator by the Missouri legislature.

So far as the scientific evidence is concerned, it will be understood, of course, that no attempt is here made to present that. The purpose is merely to call attention to some of the eminent scientists who have done notable work and to mention a few of the more interesting discoveries made. Those who desire to come into possession of the evidence in full will find upon examination that it is voluminous.

From the viewpoint of physical science alone the evidence of the continuity of consciousness is not only convincing but conclusive; yet occult science has much more to offer. To those who have no personal knowledge of the existence of occult faculties, such evidence can be offered only upon the inherent reasonableness of the statements made.

The truth of clairvoyance, like all other truths, must slowly win its way to general acceptance. While large numbers of people still scoff at it, even as the world not so very long ago scoffed at hypnotism as a fantastic theory with no foundation in fact, there is nevertheless a large and rapidly growing number who personally know the truth about clairvoyance.

Occasionally we read about occurrences that can be explained only by the hypothesis that some people are clairvoyant. This is well illustrated by a tragedy that occurred some years ago in the city of Flint, Michigan. Little Harold Moon, ten years old, mysteriously disappeared from his home in midwinter. It was thought that he might have been skating and broken through the ice. A pond not far from his home was dragged but without result and then the Flint River was likewise examined, but no trace of the missing boy could be found.

The newspapers at the time devoted columns of space to the story. At Port Huron, some forty miles away, a lady who was clairvoyant turned her attention to the matter and wrote the father of the missing boy that the dead body of his son was at the bottom of the pond above mentioned. She gave a detailed description, saying that he wore skates and that the feet were so entangled in the weeds at the bottom of the pond that the body could not rise to the surface. She described the exact location by making a diagram with lines running from surrounding trees and houses to the spot where she declared the body could be found. Again the searchers dragged the pond but found nothing. They returned to the river where they were equally unsuccessful.

Meantime the clairvoyant so insistently urged the truth of her story that at last it was decided to drain the pond. When that was done the boy's body was found at the point and in the condition described by her. Thousands of people who had been daily following the newspaper reports of the developments in the case know that the clairvoyant correctly located the body and insisted upon the accuracy of her description several days before her advice was acted upon and the truth was thus discovered. How did she know what could not be known by any physical sense?

It should be understood, of course, that clairvoyant investigations are not infallible. Clairvoyance is merely a sense, as eyesight is, and may be used with varying degrees of accuracy. As with eyesight, the observation may be either casual or careful and the deductions may be definite or vague. A clairvoyant may be mistaken for precisely the same reason that an investigator using his eyes may draw erroneous conclusions. He may not see accurately, or, having seen unerringly, he may not remember correctly when he comes to record or to repeat it. Witnesses who have observed the same incidents often go into court and flatly contradict each other as to what really occurred. One is sure that the sun was shining while another is equally sure that it was cloudy; one says a cloak was blue while another knows it was green; one refers to the distance between two objects as being but a few feet while another insists that it was as many yards. As with eyesight, so with clairvoyance. It is merely a method of consciousness which the observer uses and the correctness of his deductions depends upon the qualifications of the observer.

There are two distinct kinds of clairvoyance and that which is most in evidence with the public is not calculated to inspire confidence. It is employed almost exclusively in what is known as "fortune-telling" and is often practiced by those who are interested only in the money they can earn by it. As a matter of course, trickery and fraud are found associated with it among such people, and those amongst them who are both capable and honest suffer on account of it.

The fortune-telling clairvoyant is usually one who was born with "second sight," as the Scotch have named it, and almost without an exception they do not in the least understand its rationale. They find certain facts in their consciousness that could not be known to them by the physical senses, but why or how they get the information they do not know. That form of clairvoyance is a sensitiveness usually related to the sympathetic nervous system, the center of which is the solar plexus. It has no necessary association with intelligence, and will often be possessed by the ignorant and uncouth. It is vestigial and will slowly disappear from the race.

The higher clairvoyance, the only true "clear seeing," is associated with the cerebro-spinal nervous system and its seat is in the brain. It is not a "natural gift"* like the other, although it is latent in all human beings. It has been highly developed in some who have had the unusual opportunity of long training under the direct supervision of great psychic scientists. Such clairvoyants are never to be found among the fortune tellers. Only people with serious views of life and intense devotion to human service would have the patience and endurance to undergo such training and only those of singular purity of life would have any possibility of success. Such clairvoyants are people of keen intelligence. By special training and tremendous effort, not yet possible to most of us, they have pressed forward in evolution and attained a development that the race will be many a century in reaching.

It is true that the work of occult scientists cannot be verified by those who have no such faculties, but, as a matter of fact, we do not personally verify the pronouncements of physical science before acting upon them. Not one man in ten thousand knows himself the truth of the scientific dictums he accepts. The average man, every day of his life, acts upon information of which he personally knows nothing. He knows nothing of chemistry but he tries to avoid what he is told is chemically injurious. He does not understand surgery but trusts his life to the experts who do. He cannot distinguish quinine from strychnine, but unhesitatingly takes what the doctor gives

---

* There are, of course, really no natural gifts. Nature does not favor some and ignore others. When a few possess what others do not have, they have earned it by giving special attention to its development.

him. Many of the scientific facts he accepts are not only personally unverified but are in contradiction to the testimony of his physical senses. He believes the earth is a sphere but his personal experience is all in favor of the idea that it is flat. He believes the statement that the earth rotates upon its axis but his eyes tell him it is the sun that moves.

Few of us know of our personal knowledge the simplest facts in astronomy, or chemistry, or history, or physics. We accept the investigations of others. Even if we were not too busy to act for ourselves we should find that a certain amount of training is necessary to fit a man to be an astronomer or chemist; and so only a small number are engaged in such research. Very few people have the mental equipment essential for the work, together with the disposition to engage in it. The great scientist is a man of good intellect and almost infinite patience. He must have, also, the devotion to his work for its own sake that means complete absorption in it. This is a combination of qualities very rare in human beings and the consequence is that the vast majority of people are obliged to take scientific facts from others and use reason alone in accepting or rejecting them.

When we come to occult science the necessary qualifications of the explorer are human characteristics much rarer than those required in physical research. Any person who desires to do so may take up the study of Theosophy and quickly have the proof of its ethical truths by observing the results, in his daily life, of practicing its precepts; but the advanced explorer, the investigator in occultism, who may be compared with a trained physical scientist, must have, among other qualifications, purity of body. Such characteristics are so rare a combination that it is not strange that occult scientists are few in number; but these few, like the larger number devoted to physical science, are gradually acquiring information of great practical value to those fortunate enough to be interested. Theosophy no more asks that its truths be accepted with unquestioning credulity than physical science expects its facts to be thus received. In each case those who explore the unknown and bring back information for those who are not able to do that for themselves place before the public facts that may be verified by all who will qualify themselves for such work. Neither expects blind faith, but rather reasoning consideration. In the end it is not our personal experience but our reason upon which we rely. We do not accept things as facts solely because we have personally tested them but because our reason approves them.

It is by the use of the higher type of clairvoyance that invisible realms are explored and supplemental knowledge is added to the ancient wisdom. Such a clairvoyant is not a medium. The medium surrenders his physical mechanism for the use of another, who speaks through it, and at the close of the seance the medium knows nothing of what has been said. The clairvoyant is always in possession of his senses and is fully aware of what is occurring. He is the explorer and discoverer. He deals with the facts of the life after bodily death in a different way than the physical scientist does but it is soon found by the student that the physical scientist and the psychic scientist corroborate each other. Together they bring overwhelming evidence to support the hypothesis that life is continuous; that the consciousness we have at this moment will never cease to be; that our individuality, with all its present memories, will eternaly persist; that what we call death is in reality but a forward step in an orderly evolutionary journey and an entrance upon a more joyous phase of life. The sum total of the knowledge that we have gained through the combined work of the material scientists and the occult scientists leads us to the conclusion that the death of the physical body means neither the annihilation of consciousness nor a radical change in consciousness. It is, in fact, but the release of consciousness from its confinement to the physical form, as a songbird is released from a cage to the joyous freedom of a wider world, where woods and stream and field and sky give new impulse to its innate characteristics.

## CHAPTER V.

## THE EVOLUTIONARY FIELD

In a treatise on elementary Theosophy, the solar system may be reckoned as our universe and we shall have no need of considering more than a small fragment of that. It is septenary in constitution as may be seen by its vibrations expressed in color and sound. Beyond the seven colors of the prism, we have only tints, and outside the seven notes we can get only overtones or undertones.

The word "plane," so often encountered in theosophical literature, should perhaps be defined. It has a wide application and is used as a synonym for region, place, sphere, or world. In referring to the physical plane, the term embraces all we know of earth and sky, and life through the physical senses.

In discussing the evolutionary field, through which the soul makes its cyclic pilgrimage, only that portion of it which is invisible need engage our attention. The first thing to be said about that invisible world is that the approach to it is over familiar ground. The streetcars we ride upon and the telegrams we send are visible evidence of the existence of the invisible thing we call electricity—a force as incomprehensible to the scientist as to the schoolboy. The very winds that blow are a part of the invisible—moving masses of an invisible matter that we are now able to condense into visible, liquid form. There is a still rarer matter than air, the ether, that science declares exists, although it can not condense it, nor in any way whatever grasp, measure or contact it. How, then, is it known to exist? Because certain phenomena could not be, without it. So in air and ether we have two kinds of invisible matter, and in electricity we have a force working through one of them whose visible results we see daily.

Theosophy divides the universe into seven planes or regions of nature, but for our present purpose we need give attention to but three of them; the physical, astral and mental. On these occur all the phenomena of life and death, and a clear understanding of them will dispel all doubt and drive away all fear for either our friends or ourselves. While two of these divisions of our solar system are invisible to physical sight and impalpable to physical touch, they are, nevertheless, composed of matter, and this invisible matter interpenetrates and completely permeates all visible matter. If we could take a large sponge, very coarse and porous, of spherical shape, and completely fill every cell with very fine sand, and also surround it entirely with the sand; if this sand globe, somewhere larger than the sponge, could then be lifted, with the sponge inside, and put into a globe of water that would completely surround both while the water interpenetrated the whole mass, filling all the space between the grains of sand, that would give us a rough idea of the relationship of these three regions of nature. The sponge would represent the physical region, enveloped and interpenetrated by the sand representing the astral region. The mental region would be represented by the water which entirely surrounds and interpenetrates every particle of both the others. Holding this picture in the mind a moment, it is easy to see how a force acting on the sand and moving the grains need not in the least disturb the sponge; and how, also, force acting on the molecules of the water need not affect anything but the water, although they be moved freely through the entire mass. As a matter of fact, something approximating that is just what is occurring on these three planes of the universe. All the activities of life go forward on each without in the least interfering with any other.

These regions of nature, these grades of matter growing finer and rarer, may be crudely represented by the difference that exists between ice, water, and steam. We can take the visible solid called ice, by the application of heat raise the rate of vibration until it becomes the visible liquid called water. We can continue the process until we change the visible liquid called water into the invisible gas called steam. It is precisely the same matter all the time. We have merely raised the vibratory rate and in doing that we have caused a solid to disappear. Of course, every atom of that matter is as much in existence as though we could still see it, and if this were done in a laboratory the steam could be reduced to vapor, the vapor to water and the water to ice, giving us the identical solid with which we began.

Each plane consists of a totally different grade of matter than the next plane, but all have for their base the ultimate atom of the solar system. When modern science discovered, to its astonishment, that the physical atom was a composite body it confirmed the theosophical teaching that the ultimate chemical atom was *not* the final point of division. Theosophy teaches that when the ultimate physical atom is disintegrated its particles become the coarsest matter of the next plane or region above it—the astral plane. The process repeated with astral matter results in driving its ultimate atom from the highest level of the astral plane, or world, to the lowest of the mental plane. He who said the atom is the brick of the universe stated a great truth, for of its combinations all forms are built; and if the idea be applied to the ultimate atom of the solar system it will be true that of such "bricks" all the planes are built.

The astral plane, surrounding and interpenetrating the physical plane is, of course, an enormously larger globe and is composed of exceedingly tenuous matter. This vast sphere of invisible matter is *within* the earth as well as beyond it, interpenetrating every atom of physical matter to the earth's center. It is because its grossest grade of matter is so rare, and its vibration so intense, that they do not affect the physical senses and therefore we remain unconscious of that realm while its matter moves freely through all physical objects. We are unconscious of its life and activities for precisely the same reason that we know nothing of the messages of intelligence registered by the vibrations of the wireless telegraph, although they pass through the room where we sit. We have no sense organs with which it is possible to receive such vibrations. Messages conveying intelligence of tremendous import, involving the movements of vast armies, the fall of empires and the destinies of great nations, flow through the very space we occupy but we are wholly unconscious of them. Even so we remain blind and deaf to the stupendous activities of life and consciousness in the astral world, notwithstanding the fact that it surrounds and permeates us while its forms, unseen and unfelt, move through the physical world as freely as water flows through a sieve.

The mental plane, or world, constitutes a region of our earth still more vast than the astral portion of it. As the astral sphere encloses the physical globe, the mental encompasses both, enclosing them and also interpenetrating them to the earth's center. The term "mental world" may seem confusing to some because we are accustomed to think of the mental and the material as being opposites. The mental world, or sphere, or plane, of Theosophy, is a world of *matter,* not merely thought. It is matter, however, so remarkably tenuous that it may properly be called mind-stuff, and in its rarest levels it is said to be "formless" so far as the existence of what the physical senses know as form is concerned.

All three of these concentric globes—the physical, astral and mental—are, then, worlds of matter, of form, of activity.

If the relationship of the three worlds—physical,

astral and mental—is fully understood later confusion of thought will be avoided. Physical language is not capable of fully expressing much with which students of the occult must deal. Because there is nothing better for the purpose, words must be used that express but a part of the truth and may sometimes prove misleading unless the constitution and relationship of the three spheres is kept in mind. Thus, it is necessary to speak of higher and lower worlds, or planes, of inner or outer, and of coming "down" into the material world when, as a matter of fact, *no movement in space* is under consideration. The astral is commonly spoken of as an inner plane and we refer to coming down from higher planes to lower. That may be true not only in the sense of changing the state of consciousness from higher vibrations to lower but it *could* mean a journey in space from a point in the astral plane above the physical globe to a point at its surface or below the surface, within the earth. "Up" and "down" are relative, not absolute. "Down" for us is toward the earth's center and "up" is from the center. A spire in the Occident and a spire in the Orient are both said to be pointing upward but they are pointing in opposite directions. On most parts of the earth's surface we have four directions, while at the poles there is, of course, but one direction—south or north, as the case may be. East, west and north disappear at the north pole. Reflection upon such facts leads one to at least faintly comprehend the possibility of space itself disappearing from the inner planes—space as we know it.

The matter of each of the planes consists of seven classes. We are familiar with solids, liquids, and gases of the physical plane, and to them must be added the four grades of the ether. The seven grades of matter of the astral and mental worlds constitute an important part of the mechanism for the soul's evolution, for they determine the state of consciousness in the life beyond the physical plane. But a study of those states of consciousness belongs to a later chapter.

A difficulty which the student of Theosophy should make an early effort to eliminate is the tendency to think of invisible realms as unreal. It should not be forgotten that it is only the limitation of the physical senses that gives rise to the feeling of unreality beyond the visible.

We frequently hear people who are students of the occult speak of a deceased person as having left the earth. But passing into the astral plane, or world, is not, of course, leaving the earth. Both the astral world and the mental world are divisions of the earth. As the atmosphere is invisible and yet is a part of the earth's physical matter, so the invisible astral and mental regions are other parts of the earth. They are properly called worlds because the activities in consciousness that make up existence there are as remote from ours as though they were upon another planet. We have erroneously supposed that with the physical senses we really see and know the earth, whereas we have known only that small fragment of the earth that consists of physical matter. Beyond the limitation of our poor senses stretch in unsuspected grandeur vaster regions of our earth, swept by the vibrations of an intenser life.

## CHAPTER VI.

## THE MECHANISM OF CONSCIOUSNESS

The soul is a center of consciousness within the all-consciousness, or the life of the solar Logos. It is an individualized portion of the universal mind. That fragment of the divine life, with its latent Godlike attributes, is expressed through a complex mechanism of consciousness that is formed of the matter of the various planes. Naturally enough it is expressed more fully upon the higher planes than upon the lower. At a very high level it is known as the monad. When it reaches outward into the higher subdivisions of the mental world it is the ego, a lesser expression of the same divine life that pours from the Logos, God, through the monad—lesser because it is then functioning through the denser matter of a lower level.

The knowledge that has been gained about the nature of matter in recent years is helpful in understanding the activities of consciousness. The atom is found to be a center of force, and we are at the point where matter, as we have known it, disappears. All the force and consciousness of the solar system is, of course, but the life of the Logos, and on higher planes the distinctions we observe here fade out. Matter becomes a very different thing from the matter we know. The ether of the physical world is almost inconceivably tenuous matter; yet it is gross when compared to even the lowest grade of astral matter. The matter of the mental world is enormously rarer than the most tenuous matter of the astral world. In view of these facts it requires no stress of the imagination to understand that the matter of the higher planes is responsive to the vibrations of consciousness.

The outraying energies of the individualized center of consciousness act upon the matter of the plane and draw about it a film that slowly grows into a vehicle through which consciousness can be more fully expressed, and which serves as a point of vantage from which its expression can be extended to lower planes. A thoughtful writer has said that man is the universe in miniature. His mental and moral nature is a fragment of the supreme life. His physical being is a microscopic replica of the material universe.

Precisely as the earth has its visible and invisible regions of matter freely interpenetrating each other, so a human being has visible and invisible bodies, composed of these different grades of matter, with the same interpenetrating relationship. We have from birth not only the visible physical body, but the invisible astral, mental, and spiritual bodies; and just as the astral region of the earth not only interpenetrates the physical but extends beyond it in all directions, so the matter of the astral body interpenetrates the matter of the physical body, and extends somewhat beyond it. It is an exact duplicate in form and feature of the material body.

We must, however, guard against the misconception that such likeness is true also of the mental and spiritual bodies. The term "body" should be thought of as the mass of matter which the soul draws to itself on various planes for the purpose of expressing itself on those levels. On the higher planes it is merely a mass of the matter of those planes that differs but little from the general mass so far as form is concerned but it is individualized. On the lower mental plane form begins to appear in that mass of matter—form that is at least a suggestion of body as we commonly use that word; but it is only on the lower, not lowest, subdivision of the astral region and on the physical that we have the body as we know it in daily life. The word "body," then, this form with limbs, is applicable only for the physical and astral regions. Beyond the astral such a form would have no use, could serve no purpose. Yet on the higher mental plane we speak of a spiritual body but it is no longer the *kind* of form we see here; yet it is a form so far as function is concerned—a glorified, radiant expression of the individual we have known here in a dense material body.

To understand how the real self or conscious being comes into possession of these bodies, we must get rid of some of the delusions of which we are now the unconscious victims. One of these is that this physical life is the point where we begin the journey in the cycle of existence. This is not the home plane of the soul. It is the farthest region away from it; but on this point we are in the grip of the same sort of delusion that leads us to see the earth as the center of the universe, with the sun and stars apparently moving about it. If we could be transported to the sun, and from there behold the earth as the mote it would comparatively be, that delusion about their relative size and movement would instantly vanish. Precisely so would this illusion of the exaggerated importance of the physical plane, with its material affairs, vanish if viewed from the mental region. Indeed, so very illusory is this physical life that the occultist speaks of the physical body as the "shadow" of the real self. As we move toward the higher regions we approach reality.

Let us think of the conscious being, the living, thinking soul, as beginning its journey for a cycle of experience in the highest or rarest portion of the realm that we have called the mental region. Its desire for experience generates energy. It draws to itself the unimaginably rare matter of the mental region somewhat as a magnet attracts iron filings, and as these minute iron particles arrange themselves about the magnet in perfect order, obeying the laws of vibration with the same accuracy with which the earth moves in its orbit, so in different but analogous fashion is this mental matter drawn about the soul for the construction of the mental vehicle. This accomplished, the soul continues its descent into matter, the astral body being the next acquisition.

We must not be misled by the phrase, "descent into matter," or by the expression, "from higher down to lower regions." There is no higher or lower in the sense of altitude. The mental region is not farther away than the astral. Both are as much here as the physical. We must not lose sight of the fact that the matter of both interpenetrates all physical matter, and also completely envelops it. So the soul, or consciousness, does not come down from some place. There is no movement in space necessary. It merely attracts to itself the matter of a very rare grade, called "mental"; then, in a coarser grade of matter, the astral body is secured. Finally, by a different process, but still one of slow building, the physical body is constructed of physical matter. The three vehicles, or organisms, through which the soul is to function in the three regions are now ready to enable it to contact the various grades of matter and to obtain the experience it seeks.

Having followed in thought the way in which, starting on the home plane of the soul, we are successively clothed in the matter of these three regions, thus acquiring vehicles in which it is possible to function in each region, we are in a position to understand that this physical body is very far from being the real man; and that we are, each of us, far more than we appear to be, far more than we are able to express through this physical mechanism. A theosophical writer has used the excellent illustration of likening the soul on its home plane to the bare hand. The hand is capable of much. In music, in art, in many lines of commercial dexterity, it can work wonders. When the soul clothes itself in mental matter it is more like a hand that has put on a very thin glove. It is a limitation. The fingers are not so nimble. When, in addition, the soul takes on the astral body, it is as though the thinly gloved hand drew on a heavy glove. Now the limitation is sorely felt. The fingers can scarcely move. The delicate touch has vanished, and the enrapturing music becomes broken and uncertain. The wonderful painting is but a distortion. When the soul reaches the physical plane and begins to express itself through the physical body, this is as though over the thin and heavy glove is drawn a thick mitten. The four fingers are now one. The hand is a clumsy club, and the once divine harmony would be but meaningless sound. And thus, limited and confined as we are in dense matter, the soul is showing forth in this visible life but the merest fragment of the real self.

Each of these bodies serves as a vehicle of consciousness on the plane to which it belongs. The soul is evolving simultaneously in each of the worlds, physical, astral, and mental, and these various bodies enable it to receive the vibrations of the plane they belong to and thus to be conscious there. The mental body is the seat of intellectual activity. Thought arises as a vibration in it and passes through the astral body into the physical brain. Whenever we think, we are using the mental body. The astral body is the seat of emotion. With it we feel. All emotion passes from it to the physical body to be expressed in the material world. The astral world is also called the emotional world, as the mental plane is called the heaven world. The physical body is the soul's instrument of action. It attaches it to the physical world, enables the consciousness to contact material objects and to move about and express on the material plane the thoughts and emotions generated in the mental and astral bodies. It should be kept in mind that these two invisible vehicles surround and interpenetrate the physical body.

Another part of the mechanism of consciousness is known as the etheric double; but it is only a link in the chain and not a body through which the soul can function. It is composed of the etheric matter of the physical world and connects the astral body with the physical body. As every atom of physical matter is surrounded and permeated by etheric matter, it follows that the physical body has its duplicate in etheric matter. "Etheric double" is a very appropriate name since it is a perfect duplicate of the physical body in etheric matter. It serves the purpose of supplying the life force to the nervous system and is the medium through which sensation is conveyed. The action of an anesthetic drives out so much of the matter of the etheric double that the connection is broken and sensation in the physical body ceases.

One of the difficulties in the way of getting a clear conception of the constitution of man, and realizing that he is a soul functioning through various vehicles of consciousness, is the materialistic modes of thought common to Occidental civilization. We are accustomed to thinking of the physical body itself as being the man, and if there is any thought at all of the consciousness surviving the death of the body it is very vague and indefinite as to where it exists and how it is expressed. Very little thinking should be necessary to show the absurdity of the belief that the body is the man. Two bodies may be alike, as in the case of twins, but the souls, the real men, may be absolutely unlike. The real man is superphysical. His intelligence or his stupidity, his genial disposition or his moroseness, his generosity or his selfishness, are but the manifestations of himself through the body by which they are expressed. The body itself is a mere aggregation of physical atoms, as a planet is, so organized that they constitute an instrument for a purpose. The mass of matter constituting the body is a variable mass. It may increase or diminish greatly, but the man remains unchanged. There is no permanent relationship between the man and the physical matter which he uses for his vehicle of consciousness. According to the physiologists every atom of the body changes within a period of a few years. The cells wear out, break down and pass away to be replaced by new matter. Not a particle of the physical matter that was in our bodies a few years ago is there now, and none that is there now will remain. Within a very few years we shall have bodies composed of new matter as certainly as an infant's is.

This constant changing of the matter that constitutes the material body goes steadily on day and night during our lifetime. In some parts of the body it is very slow while in other parts it is so rapid that every person has proof of the fact that the body he has today is not composed of the matter that was his body a very few years ago. We know, for example, that the matter in the finger nails changes so fast that we have to continually file it away. We know that the hair that covered a man's head five years ago is not the same hair he has now. It is stated in Cutter's Physiology, one of our popular school books, that all the matter in the physical body is renewed within a period of seven years. The occult scientists say that the complete renewal occurs within a much shorter time. Atom by atom the new matter is built in, true to the existing matrix at any given moment. The form of a mole or scar remains. Only the matter that constitutes it is changed. In advanced years we lose vitality. The body is no longer able to expel the effete matter and the limbs stiffen.

Of course such reconstruction of the body does not change its appearance. It is built on the same lines. It is as it would be with some very old building. As the centuries pass it must be slowly rebuilt. The floors wear out and are relaid. The roof serves its time and is replaced. The walls crumble first in one place and then another until they have been completely reconstructed. After a thousand years have passed there may be none of the original material in the building, yet its appearance is unchanged. In a few years the matter composing the bodies we have today will have passed away and will be growing in the trees and blooming in the flowers. The matter of the bodies we shall then have is now scattered through the world. It will be brought together during that time and will come from many parts of the earth.

The physical senses continually deceive us and nowhere more than in our ideas about the physical body. It is an unstable mass of matter, in constant motion, with much space between its atoms. Emerson was very far ahead of his time and it took science more than a half century to catch up with him and learn that he had recorded a fact in nature when he wrote:

> Atom from atom yawns as far
> As earth from moon, or star from star.

In 1908 the *Scientific American Supplement,* commenting on our reconstructed ideas about matter, remarked that the actual mass of the physical body to the apparent mass is about one to one million!

Clearly, the physical body is not the man. If it were, the loss of a part of the body would logically be a loss of part of the man; but we know he may lose both arms and both lower limbs, the sight of both eyes, the hearing, the major part of the lungs and the entire stomach, and still live his allotted time. With so little of the physical body left he is the same man, with all the force of will and power of thought, with all the attributes of character, that constitute a human being. This mere fragment of a body is sufficient for the real man to function through in the visible world. Of course, there is a point beyond which the mutilation of the physical organism cannot go without forcing the ego to abandon it; but every forward step in surgery is demonstrating more and more clearly that the body is but a wonderful machine and laboratory operated by a still more wonderful and independent intelligence —the soul, the self. If the physical body is merely

## The Mechanism of Consciousness

an organized mass of matter, continually varying, constantly coming and going, and having no permanent relationship to the consciousness that functions through it, what reason is there for believing that it is the man?

This complex mechanism of consciousness, composed of the various bodies through which the ego expresses itself at different levels, is used as a whole for functioning on the physical plane; but when the ego is functioning no farther down than the astral plane, the physical body is, of course, temporarily discarded. It is then in the condition known as sleep, or trance. Sleep is the natural withdrawing of the consciousness from the physical body. When the separation occurs in the case of the medium it is called trance. The physical body in sleep is unoccupied, but the consciousness maintains magnetic connection with it. In death that tie is severed and the consciousness can return to the body no more. Instances in which the apparently dead are brought back to life are cases where the magnetic tie is not broken, notwithstanding there is every appearance of death.

In form and feature the physical body has its exact duplicate in the astral body which surrounds and interpenetrates the physical body, and in the astral body we function in the astral world whenever the separation between the two occurs, whether from sleep or death. In sleep the consciousness, expressing itself in the astral body in the astral world, may be turned dreamily inward or it may be turned outward and be vividly aware of the life and activities of that world; but there is small chance that any memory of it will come through into the physical consciousness upon awakening. Occasionally, however, it does occur and then it is usually remembered as a very vivid dream. In illness, and other abnormal conditions, the connection between the physical and astral consciousness is much closer. At a comparatively high point in evolution the two states of consciousness merge. The man is then continuously conscious, and has a full memory in the physical brain of all his activities in the astral world during the hours when the physical body was asleep.

Consciousness is, of course, at its worst when expressed through the limitation of its lower vehicles. Any person, whether brilliant or stupid, will be much abler and keener on the astral plane than on the physical, because in sleep, as after death, he has lost the limitations imposed by physical matter. But the degree of restriction is variable and depends much upon the *kind* of matter of which the brain and body are composed; for the physical atoms vary greatly, and as they come and go in the passing years the body may either become purified and refined or it may grow grosser and coarser. By careful attention to character building, by control of the emotions, the limitations of physical matter may be lessened and a much higher and more efficient state of consciousness in the physical body can be attained.

## CHAPTER VII.

## DEATH

Perhaps one of the reasons why death is so commonly associated with a feeling of fear is because we give so little thought to it. Most people seem never to think of the subject at all until death invades the home or threatens some member of the family. Then terror fills the mind and all but paralyzes the reasoning faculties.

Such fear of death, so widespread in Occidental civilization, is eloquent testimony to the materialism of our times. It is doubt about the future that causes fear of death. Only when we have a scientific basis for the hope of immortality will that awful horror disappear. Death is feared because it seems like annihilation. If people really believed in a heavenly existence beyond the physical life they could not possibly be filled with terror at the prospect of entering it. If a man's religion has not given him a genuine confidence in a future life, and made it as much of a reality to him as this life is, it has failed to do what we have a right to demand of religion. If it does not enable him to look upon the face of his dead without a doubt or a fear, there is something wrong, either with his religion or with his comprehension of it. What possible reason is there for fearing death? A thing that is universal, that comes to all, can not be pernicious. To regard death as a disastrous thing would be an indictment of the sanity of nature.

Death is merely the close of a particular cycle of experience. It is the annihilation of nothing but the physical body, in its role of an instrument of activity and a vehicle of the consciousness upon the physical plane. The atoms of the body, drawn together in the human form for temporary use are, in death, released from the cohesive force of a living organism and will return whence they came.

In reality there is no such thing as death, unless it be strictly applied to the form, regarded as a temporary medium of consciousness. As for the consciousness, there is no death. There is life in a physical form and life out of it, but no such thing as the death, or cessation, of the individual intelligence. What we name "death" is but a stage in the orderly evolution of life, and it is only because the phenomenon is viewed from the physical plane that such a term can be applied to it. From this plane it is death or departure; but looked at from the astral world it is birth, or arrival. What we call birth is the beginning of the expression of the soul through a material body on the physical plane. It is an arrival. But from the inner or higher viewpoint it is a departure and therefore is as logically a "death" there as departure from a physical body is here. So death and departure from one plane is simply birth, or arrival, upon another, although it is not, of course, birth as we know it.

Every process in nature has a part to play in evolution and therefore death is as necessary as life and as beneficial as birth. Death is the destroyer of the useless. There is a time when each human being should die—that is to say, a time when the physical body has fulfilled its mission and completely accomplished the purpose for which it exists. To continue life in a physical body beyond that point is to waste energy and lose time in the evolutionary journey. Under the action of what we call "disease" the body becomes inefficient, or through its gradual breaking down in old age the senses grow dim and uncertain. The consciousness can no longer be keenly expressed through its impaired machine and it is decidedly to the advantage of the ego to withdraw from it. The soul is in the position of an artisan obliged to work with broken and rusted tools. Good results are no longer possible. It is then that death comes, beneficently destroying the worn-out instrument and releasing the consciousness from its too-often painful situation and permitting its escape into the astral plane.

Death is painless. The breaking down of the body under the ravages of disease may cause pain, but that belongs to physical life, not to death. Distress may also be caused by groundless fear of death; but the dying person who does not know that death is upon him has no terror, and no pain, and sinks quietly to sleep. Very little observation will convince one that the distress about a deathbed is invariably on the part of surviving friends, not on the part of the dying.

Those who are left behind remain within the limitations of the physical senses, and they are therefore separated from the so-called dead man, but he is not separated from them. It is because of that separation that the terror of death exists for them; but in that very fact is to be seen the great evolutionary value of death. The separation it causes intensifies love as nothing else could do. It is usually when our friend is gone that we begin to appreciate his real value and comprehend how large a part he really played in our existence. As sudden silence gives us a keener realization of a sound that has just ceased, so death, by its contrast, gives a vivid, realistic touch to life. We all know how enormously the heart qualities are quickened by the death of a close friend. The whole nature is in some degree purified and spiritualized. Selfishness decreases and compassion grows. Sympathy for others in distress is born, and thus a decided evolutionary advance is made.

We have only to reflect upon the fact that separation without death produces the same effects in a minor key, to realize the evolutionary value of death. In constant association we grow careless and indifferent; but an absence of a month or two enables one to get a truer perspective of personal associations and thereafter life has new zest. A child regards its mother with a certain degree of appreciation; but a short absence enormously increases its valuation of her presence. All human beings come into closer and more sympathetic association after a period of separation, and the completeness of the separation caused by death renders it peculiarly efficacious in the development of the spiritual side of one's nature.

It often requires death to turn attention away from materialistic life. Frequently a family becomes completely absorbed in material success. There is no thought at all given to the higher life. Wealth, position, power, fame, all the vanities of the world, firmly hold them. They become completely self-centered. Then suddenly death enters and breaks the family circle, and the transient character of all they had been so strenuously striving for suddenly dawns upon them, and attention is turned to the nobler things of life. It is a well-known fact that great wars are accompanied or followed by widespread spiritual awakening, and it is no doubt largely because the shadow of death has fallen on tens of thousands of homes.

It has sometimes been asked by doubting critics if it would not be an improvement on nature's plan if the sorrow caused by the death of our friends were softened by direct knowledge of their continued existence. It is evidently the plan of nature to have the physical life and the astral life normally separated at our present level of evolution. Some of the reasons have already been discussed. There are undoubtedly others that we are incapable of understanding, and still others that we can readily comprehend. If the higher, joyous life of the astral world were open to our consciousness, then concentration upon the duties of this life would be difficult, if not impossible. Our life in the physical body may be compared to the tasks of children in school. They have serious business before them in the acquiring of knowledge and the development of the intellect. They can best accomplish the work when completely isolated from other phases of life. Introduce daily into their work-day the joys of a child's existence, the circus, the military parade, the picnic, the dancing parties, and the purpose for which the school exists would be defeated. To exactly the extent that the consciousness is withdrawn from such things will desirable progress be made with the work of the schoolroom. And so it is with the limitation of our physical senses. It serves a purpose.

However, there is a point in human evolution where such limitations of the senses is no longer of any service and may be transcended. Some people have attained it. There are those who have previously been referred to as the psychic scientists, with the higher clairvoyance of the cerebro-spinal nervous system developed. It is an accomplishment to which all may aspire. None need submit to the separation commonly caused by death. By hard work in co-operating with nature's methods of evolution and by a serious and sustained effort to live the highest and most helpful life of which one is capable, it is possible in time to attain a level of consciousness where one has personal knowledge that the dead still live.

One of the common delusions about death is that some radical change in the nature of a person then takes place. This is no doubt due in part to the theological ideas that have come down to us from the

# Death

Middle Ages. It is thought by many that at death one comes to some sort of judgment that classes him as either a saint qualified for eternal bliss or a fiend fit only for endless torture! The belief is based on that erroneous view of human nature that was common to the melodrama of a past generation. It represented the hero as unqualifiedly good and the villain as absolutely bad. The one had no flaw of character and the other had not a redeeming virtue. But human nature does not thus express itself. The spark of divine life is in all, notwithstanding it is sometimes darkly hidden. On the other hand we find about us no perfected beings. The perfect heroes are merely creations of an imperfect imagination. At our halfway stage of evolution we find neither the absolutely good nor the hopelessly bad though a few have risen very high in moral development and a few have sunk into bestial characteristics from which they can rise only with great difficulty.

Why should the change we call death transform a human being? It is merely the loss of one part of the mechanism of consciousness. The soul, the thinker, has lost connection with the material world because the physical body has ceased to exist. The mental body and the astral body remain and they enable him to think and feel. But he cannot think more than he knows, nor feel what he has not evolved. All that has happened in death is that contact with the material world has been lost.

One of the misconceptions is that death brings great wisdom, and we often hear of people communicating with those who have passed on, with the hope of obtaining valuable advice. It is true that death ushers one into a realm of wider consciousness, but—and it is a vital point—he would have no better judgment in determining a course of action than he had while here in the physical world.

Both mentally and emotionally he is unchanged. His grade of morality is neither better nor worse. His tolerance or narrowness remains what it previously was. If he was bigoted while here he is still intolerant there. If he was the unevolved ignoramus here he remains precisely that in the astral world. Whether genius or fool, saint or villain, he remains unchanged and goes on with his evolutionary development, but in a world where emotion is the ruling factor.

Death merely opens the door to a new and wider realm where our evolution proceeds. It would be difficult to say which is the greater misfortune— the delusions that make death the king of terrors, or the complacent belief that if death does not end all, it at least brings the soul to a judgment that ends all personal responsibility and settles one's fate forever. Death can no more lessen responsibility or transform the moral nature than sleep can change character or determine destiny.

The theosophical conception of the matter is as consoling as it is scientific. Instead of the fear of death it gives us knowledge of continued life. Instead of doubt and despair it gives us confidence and joy, for it guarantees the companionship once more of those we have known and loved but have not permanently lost.

CHAPTER VIII.

## THE ASTRAL LIFE

To those accustomed to thinking of the dying as passing to some remote heaven, where they become angels, it will perhaps sound startling to say that a "dead" man is not usually aware at first that the change we call death has taken place; yet that is a common experience. Nor is it at all remarkable that it should be so. We have only to recall the fact that all physical matter is surrounded and permeated with astral matter to realize that the physical plane is duplicated in that astral matter. Not only the physical body of the human being but, of course, every physical object, has its astral duplicate. The "dead" man sees, then, the duplicate, in astral matter, of the familiar scenes he has left behind. He sees, too, his living friends, for their astral bodies are replicas of their physical forms.

And yet, notwithstanding all this there is a difference, though not a difference that enables him to comprehend what has occurred. He may know that only yesterday, or what seems to him to have been yesterday, he was ill and confined to his bed, and was perhaps told that he was about to die; and now he is not ill; indeed, he never felt so free from aches and pains in all his life. The pulsing energies and exhilaration of youth are his again! This mystifies him. He sees his friends and naturally speaks to them, but gets no reply and finds that he cannot attract their attention. It must be remembered that he cannot see their physical bodies just as they cannot see his astral body; yet he truly sees them. If a so-called dead man and a living person look at the same instant at another living person they will both see him, but the latter sees the physical body while the former sees only the astral body that surrounds and permeates it.

Under these circumstances it is not strange that the new arrival in the astral world has a feeling of baffling mystery. He is in full possession of his reasoning faculties and will power, but there is a puzzling limitation to his efforts to produce expected results. A partial analogy may be found in the case of a person suddenly stricken with aphasia over night. He rises in the morning, dresses, and goes about his accustomed duties without the slightest suspicion that any change has come to him; but when he takes up the morning paper he finds to his amazement that the familiar print simply means nothing to him. He is all the more alarmed because there *seems* to be nothing at all wrong with him! He only knows that yesterday he could read but that today he cannot and the reason is an utter mystery. It is not difficult to imagine that he is both puzzled and alarmed. Quite as baffling and appalling must be the first experience of many who pass into the astral life without some knowledge of it. Of course, in time, the living dead man gets adjusted to the new life. He meets others in the astral world who have been there longer and they, sooner or later, succeed in convincing him that he is not having an exceptionally vivid dream.

There is a mistaken idea that the astral world is something vague, misty and unreal. In truth it is a more vivid and realistic life than this we are now living. There is nothing ghostly about it. With the shifting of the consciousness to the astral grade of matter the astral world becomes as real as the physical is now. We do not, by death, suddenly acquire great knowledge and wisdom, as is sometimes supposed, but the mind is no longer hampered by the dense physical brain. We also leave physical pain behind. There is no bodily weariness in the astral life.

Naturally enough, we cannot even imagine what so great a change means. We may think of a lifelong dungeon prisoner being suddenly released here in this world and all its prized freedom and opportunity becoming an instantaneous possession; but so tame a comparison is of little assistance. In many ways that do not occur to us larger freedom and new vistas of existence must appear. Of those that do occur to us we can hardly hope to get a comprehensive idea. Take one simple fact as an illustration—the fact that food, clothing and shelter would no longer be a problem of life, and that all the tremendous energy now given to their production would be necessarily turned in other directions. Think what that would mean if applied even to the physical life, and what a change would be wrought if each were free to use his time as he chose! Of course, the astral existence means different things to different people. We shall doubtles enjoy it or dislike it in proportion that we have wisely or foolishly lived the physical life. If we have been students we shall probably find our chief pleasure in pursuing our studies under immensely better facilities. If we have lived useful, helpful lives, we shall find wider opportunity for continuing in that line. If we have been completely absorbed in the accumulation of property, we shall probably find the sudden cutting off of all business affairs a great annoyance. If we have lived so selfishly that we cannot use our leisure and enjoy our liberty when it comes, we may find the astral world very dull and irksome.

The astral life is not punitive, but purgative. All of nature's processes are really kind and beneficent, although it is not always apparent on the surface. Pain is a friend. It is always the lesser of two evils. It is nature's danger signal. We unconsciously get the hand too close to the fire and are startled with a burn. That is merely a warning; but for it the hand would have been consumed. We overwork, and a warning pain springs up in the brain or heart. The network of nerves that makes us suffer is nature's telegraph system prepared to send an instantaneous message of warning from every point of the body to the brain. For precisely the same reason that we suffer here we may suffer there—not because we are being punished, but because the moral nature is being purged; because we are getting rid of certain traits and tendencies that to retain would mean greater suffering in the future. If a man has an abscess it may be painful to submit to the surgeon's knife; but that suffering is the way back to good health, plus the consequence of having violated some of nature's laws. There is no such thing as escape from natural law. It operates as unerringly and as exactly in the unseen world as in the visible, and therefore a study of the subject is important. By having a knowledge of the astral life and the after-death conditions, both terror and suffering may be avoided. Such suffering as may be experienced is not, of course, physical, for the physical body, with all its aches and pains, has been left behind. But we all know from experience that physical pain causes less suffering than mental and emotional distress. No physical pain is comparable to the pangs of remorse, or to the suffering caused by the sudden loss of a very dear friend. Strong but ungratified desire may also be a source of suffering, as in the case of a hard drinker here being unable to gratify his insatiable thirst. This must be equally true, in varying degree, of all other material desires which people carry with them into the astral life, where there is no possibility of their gratification.

The astral region has seven subdivisions and our location there depends upon the sort of life we live here; not that we are sorted out and assigned to different regions, as the guests at a hotel are sent to various floors, but our life here is constantly drawing into the astral body finer or coarser astral matter, and this determines with absolute accuracy our astral career. If, for example, a man lives a very low and bestial, or a very selfish life, he is thereby constantly attracting into his astral body the grossest grade of astral matter, and the preponderance of this matter will carry him to the most undesirable subplane of our world, the lower astral region, as certainly as a gross impulse here will take him where it may be gratified. This lowest subdivision of the astral world is described by trained occult observers as appearing devoid of all that is light and beautiful. One investigator describes it as having an atmosphere of grossness and loathsomeness that gives one the sensation of being surrounded by some black, viscous fluid, instead of by pure air. This is that subdivision of the astral world that is undoubtedly the basis of descriptions of purgatory or hell.

It is the next rarer region of the astral plane to which the great majority go at death, and here the sojourn may be long or short. It will depend wholly upon circumstances, precisely as the length of the physical life depends upon many things, including the soundness of the body, the care we take of it and the manner in which we live. Some may remain on the astral plane a very short time, and others for a long period. There is a much greater variation of the period spent in the astral region than on the physical plane. Here but few people live a century while large numbers die in infancy. On the astral plane nobody dies. A few pass on almost immediately, or at least very soon, to the blissful life of the mental plane, the heaven world. They are those who have lived unselfishly or nobly and usefully. Others of a fairly high type may have twenty or more years of astral life. The determining factor is the amount of gross astral matter still lingering in the emotional body and the way in which the person lives after arrival. If he is unfortunately of a gross type with little or no desire to improve he may greatly prolong his sojourn on the lowest level of the astral world. The period may even run into a few centuries.

The astral region, as a whole, is the world of desires, passions and emotions. During physical life we have generated certain forces that have not had their full expression, and this stored-up energy must work itself out on the invisible planes. It may happen that, although a man who dies has no physical body through which he can suffer, he passes through a purgative process that we should as earnestly seek to avoid as we would try to avoid burns and bruises, regrets and heartaches here. All evil and selfish thoughts and acts indulged during the physical life must necessarily cause more or less suffering in the astral life. All hatred, envy, jealousy, anger, and all gross desires and appetites indulged here must inevitably work out injuriously there. On the other hand, those who have lived clean, wholesome and unselfish lives here pass quickly to the loftiest conditions of the astral world, and for the simple reason that they have been unconsciously all the time attracting the rarest grade of astral matter to their astral bodies until it predominates.

When the astral life is finished—that is to say, when the forces that hold us to the astral plane are exhausted—we pass into the mental region, or heaven world, which is the second division of the invisible world about us. This does not represent a movement in space, but a gradual release from the astral body and a transfer of the consciousness to the mental body.

Each of these planes of nature, the physical, astral and mental, has its particular purpose in evolution. Here in the physical plane we generate certain forces which, later on, must have either good or bad results. It is, so to speak, a seed time. The astral is the purgative plane, where detrimental tendencies are worn away and undesirable forces are exhausted. The mental plane is the place of assimilation, the harvest time, the period in which we reap the rich reward of noble thought and deed and garner the wisdom from all the experiences we have passed through on the other planes. There, in a perfectly blissful life, in a state of ecstacy impossible to describe, is passed a comparatively long period. Just as on the astral plane, the circumstances once more determine the length of the life in the heaven world, but the investigators agree that in general it is a period equal to several times the length of the combined physical and astral periods. This is a time of rest and of mental and spiritual growth. All the highest aspirations of one's life on the physical plane have their complete working out. Experience becomes wisdom and power for future accomplishment. All the grossness of every possible kind has dropped away during the astral life, and not a single shadow of any sort remains to mar this life of perfect joy.*

The astral world, as previously explained, has

---

\* For a very complete detailed description of the mental plane (the heaven world) see *The Devachanic Plane* by C. W. Leadbeater.

## THE ASTRAL LIFE

seven subdivisions and the astral body contains matter belonging to each of them. While we have the physical body the matter of the astral body is in rapid circulation, every grade of it being constantly represented at the surface. But when the connection with the material plane is broken, a rearrangement of the matter of the astral body automatically takes place (unless it is prevented by an exercise of will power) and the grossest grade of matter thereafter occupies its surface. Consequently the consciousness of the man is limited to that subdivision of the astral world represented by the lowest grade of matter which his astral body contains at the time of his death.

There are three, and only three modes of death, or release from the physical body—by old age, by disease, or by violence. Old age is the natural and desirable close of the chapter of physical plane experience. It is most desirable to live to ripe old age and accumulate a large harvest of experience. To live long and actively is excellent fortune. It is not well to pass into the astral world with strong physical desires. As old age comes on the desire forces subside. Most of that grade of astral matter that is capable of expressing them has gradually disappeared. Old age represents the most gradual loosening of the life forces from the material plane, and that has many advantages.

Release from the physical form by disease is next in order of desirability. It is a quicker and less complete breaking down of the connection with the physical world. Nevertheless it is a condition in which much progress may be made in getting free from physical desires, as those who have had experience with invalids are aware. Desires naturally grow weaker with the progress of the disease that finally ends in death.

Release from the physical form by violence is, of course, the least desirable of the three, not merely because it is violence, but for the much more important reason that sudden death, excepting the elderly, finds a man, as a rule, with a considerable amount of the lower grades of astral matter in his astral body.

Whether the death by violence is the result of accident, suicide, murder, or legal execution, the astral plane conditions of consciousness are alike unfortunate, in that it is sudden death, not the manner of death, that permits entry upon the invisible life before the lower grades of astral matter have been eliminated from the emotional body. This is one reason why suicide is unfortunate—because it ushers the man into the inner world with more of the matter of the lower levels in his astral vehicle than would be there if he had lived out his normal physical life.

Purgatory is a term often applied to the lowest level of the astral world. The word is well chosen because it is there that the moral nature is purged of its impurities. Strong desires cultivated and indulged during the life in the physical body are eliminated with the gross astral matter through which alone they can be expressed and, freed to that extent, the man passes to the next subdivision, and into its higher state of consciousness.

In the astral life some people linger long on the lower levels while others know them not at all, but awaken to the blissful consciousness of one of the higher subdivisions. Nature is everywhere consistent, grouping together people of a kind. It is the manner in which one lives during physical life that determines his happiness or sorrow after death. The astral body, the seat of the emotions, is, like the physical body, constantly changing the matter that composes it. An emotion of any kind expresses itself as a vibration in the matter of the astral body. If it is a base emotion, such as anger, hatred, lust or cruelty, it throws into vibration the grossest of the astral body's matter, for only in that can it be expressed. If it is an exalted emotion, such as love, sympathy, devotion, courage or benevolence, it affects only the rarer grades of astral matter, for in them only can such feeling be expressed.

With most people there is a constant mingling of a wide range of emotions, with a gain in one direction and a loss in the other. One who fortunately understands the law of emotional cause and effect may make absolutely certain of a comfortable sojourn upon the astral plane after death. He would make it a rule to watch his emotions and control them, knowing that each time he indulged in a gross one the vibration set up in his astral body would strengthen and vivify the grossest grade of matter in it, while pure and exalted emotions would strengthen the higher grades. Ultimately, the grossest grade, becoming atrophied through inactivity, would drop away from him.

The descriptions of purgatory given by the psychic scientists are calculated to induce even the reckless to avoid it. If we could bring together all the worst men and women now living on the physical plane, the most cruel of murderers, the most besotted drunkards, the vilest degenerates, the most conscienceless and vindictive fiends of every description, huddle them together in vile hovels, and let them remain without any outward government, free to prey upon each other, we should perhaps have some comprehension of the reality of the lowest subdivision of the astral world. But no physical plane comparison can do it full justice, for we must remember that it is the emotional world and that the feelings of its inhabitants make its atmosphere in a way that would be here impossible. Astral matter instantly and exactly reproduces emotion, so that the fiend or the sensualist looks exactly what he feels. Even in unresponsive physical matter, the evil in a man is often sufficiently expressed to fill those who behold him with terror. In the astral world every cruel thought and hideous emotion would express itself in visible form. Add to this the fact that the hopeless despair of its denizens gives an atmosphere of utter gloom and desolation, and we have a hell that leaves no need of "lakes of fire" to check the course of the erring soul; and yet there is no suffering that is not self-created. It is both consistent and just that a man should associate with his kind and look upon himself in others until he grows sick of his own vileness and cries out in agony of spirit against his own moral offenses. It must not be assumed that every person dying with considerable matter belonging to the lower astral level still within his emotional body will necessarily pass through such experiences. It should never be forgotten that we are dealing with a subject of the utmost complexity and that even the most exhaustive description in print would present only a fragment of the truth. The conditions of consciousness on any subplane vary as individuals vary. Many people on the lowest astral level are wholly unconscious of their surroundings. Another variation is that some people find themselves floating in darkness and largely cut off from others—a sufficiently undesirable condition, and yet better than the fate of some. All states of astral consciousness are reactions from previous good or evil conduct and are, moreover, temporary conditions that will in time be left behind.

In a different way and at a higher level there may be suffering on the astral plane that is purifying the nature. Not all offences against nature's laws are of so gross a type. There is the foolish strengthening of desire and the violation of conscience that may result in various kinds of regret and emotional distress. A desire of a refined type strongly built up upon the physical plane lives with an intenser vitality on the astral plane after the physical body can no longer gratify it. A glutton and a miser have strong desires of very different type. Each of them is likely to suffer on account of it during the astral life. They need not dwell upon the lowest level to get a reaction from their folly in the physical life. We can easily imagine the distress of the glutton in a world without food. There could be no distress because of hunger, for the astral body is not, like the physical body, renewed and maintained by what it consumes; but hunger and the gratification of the sense of taste are very different things. It is the latter that would trouble the gormand, and it is said that suffering, as in the case of the drunkard, is his lot until the desire gradually disappears because of the impossibility of its gratification.

The miser represents a subtler form of desire, but his greed for gold may be quite as intense as that of the glutton for sensual gratification. The accumulation of money has been the dominant thought of his life. He has created in his mind a wholly false value for money and it gives him real pain to part with any of it. Only dire necessity forces him to spend any portion of his hoard. It is not difficult to imagine his emotions when he is obliged to leave it behind and see others spend it freely!

Any kind of desire that is related to the physical body is without means of gratification in the astral world and if such desire has been cultivated until it becomes strong enough to play an important part in one's life it will certainly give him more or less trouble after the loss of the physical body. Whether it grows out of an over-refinement and excess in a natural appetite, as in the case of the epicure, or is simply an artificial thing that is unrelated to any natural demand, as in the case of the smoker, the inability to gratify the desire is equally distressing. The suffering that results could hardly be judged by what would follow on the physical plane when desire is thwarted, for in the astral life emotion expresses itself much more intensely.

All of the suffering in the astral world, of whatever type, is the natural result of the thoughts, emotions and acts during the life on the physical plane. The astral world is a part of the mechanism for man's evolution that brings him up with a sharp turn when he is moving in the wrong direction. He is not being punished. The injurious forces he has generated are simply reacting upon him and they work out in a multiplicity of ways. One of the methods of reaction that helps to stamp out a fault is the automatic repetition of the unpleasant consequences of wrong doing. The murderer will serve for a general illustration. In the case of a deliberate, premeditated and cruel murder, the assassin is moved by such base motives as revenge or jealousy. The results of these, so far as their frightful consequences to the victim are concerned, do not in the least tend to deter the assassin from further deeds of violence. He feels gratified with his success and is quite satisfied with himself. Only the possibility of detection and punishment troubles him. If they follow in due course they may accomplish something in correcting his erroneous views of life; but they will not be sufficient to register indelibly, in the very nature of the man, a proper sense of the crime of which he has been guilty. Such a man can be impressed and his viewpoint changed only by consequences to himself. It is in the reaction, in the astral life, of the forces he has generated here that he gets the lesson that drives in upon his consciousness the horror inseparable from murder. If he escapes the physical plane consequences of his deed he will nevertheless come into contact in the astral world with conditions sufficiently terrifying. He has made a tie with his victim that cannot be broken until the scales of justice are balanced and nature's exaction has been paid to the uttermost. Just what form of retribution will follow depends, of course, on the nature of the case; but the reaction is as certain as it is multiplex. In the case of a murderer who has been apprehended, tried, condemned and executed, the whole of the tragedy and its sequel would be not only lived over in imagination but repeated automatically, in fact, and worked out in detail in the plastic matter of the astral region. Probably few of us have the imagination to comprehend what the murderer feels of fear at his trial, when his life is in the balance; or what he suffers while hiding from justice and making futile efforts to escape the pursuing officers of the law; or what his emotions are as his hands are tied and he steps upon the death trap. All this is reproduced in the astral life, repeatedly. As one whose mind is completely filled with a subject—let us say something that is the cause of much anxiety—finds it impossible to turn his attention from it and think of other things, or to go to sleep, and is impelled against his desire to think the matter over and over, so the assassin is enmeshed in the emotion-web of his crime and can not escape from living and acting it all over and over again and again until a revulsion of feeling arouses him to full comprehension of the horror of his crime.

Again it should be said that no attempt is here made to give more than a fragmentary description, and a few hints, of the manner in which the retributory laws of nature work. A writer on the subject should also be careful that, in pointing out the fact that to certain classes of offenders against nature's laws severe penalties accrue, the reader does not get the impression that suffering is the common lot in the astral life. The truth of the matter is that people who live clean, moderate lives, and refrain from generating forces that are injurious to others, will know nothing whatever of the unfortunate side of astral existence. In the limitations, the vexations, the physical aches and ills, the poverty, sorrow and suffering of the material plane, most of us are as near to hell-conditions of existence as we ever shall be. The kindly man of average morality has so little of the matter of the lowest level of the astral plane lingering in him that as a rule he would begin his postmortem existence on the next higher subdivision, which is the counterpart of the earth's surface. He would therefore have no knowledge of the hell that exists on the lower level; but that is not at all true of those who live grossly and freely indulge the emotions of anger, jealousy, hatred, revenge, and their kindred impulses, that often lead to violent crimes. It is possible to live the physical life so sanely, usefully, harmoniously and unselfishly that at the death of the physical body one will pass almost immediately to a joyous and useful career in the astral world; but while that is quite possible the unfortunate fact is that a great many people so color all their emotions with selfishness that the astral sojourn is unhappily affected by it. It is the emotions that determine the astral life and if they are narrowly selfish they bring the man into conditions on the astral plane that are very unpleasant.

It must be expected that any idea we may form of the astral life will be incomplete, and inadequate to give a true conception of what it is really like. Perhaps the most comprehensible of the subplanes is that which reproduces the physical landscape in astral matter. There the average man will begin his conscious astral career. If we think of the world as we know it here and then imagine all that is material to have vanished from it we shall gain some comprehension of the situation. Eliminate the necessity of providing food, clothing and shelter and nearly all of the labor of the race would cease. The tilling of the soil, the mining, the building, the manufacturing, and the transportation and exchange of products of field and factory, constitute nearly the whole of human activity. In the astral life no food is required and one is clothed with the astral matter from which garments are fashioned with the ease and rapidity of thought. No houses are needed for shelter. The astral body is not susceptible to degrees of heat and cold, and nothing there corresponds to our temperatures.

If we could drop out of physical life all need of physical labor, abolish all response to heat or cold, the need of food and houses, and give each person the ability to possess all that wealth can confer and much that it cannot, we would have an approach to a conception of the astral world from one viewpoint. Each one entering the astral life has a fullness of liberty and freedom from responsibility that is not instantly comprehensible to the physical consciousness. There is nothing whatever that he must do. There is, however, much that he can do if he desires to be active. On the physical plane many people of wealth travel and amuse themselves with sight seeing. Thousands of others would do so if it were possible. In the astral world it *is* possible, and large numbers of people drift about with no particular plans.

As the astral life becomes more and more familiar to the newly arrived individual he gets well settled in it and gradually readjusts his viewpoint to a truer perspective. As time passes he is less and less in touch with the affairs of the physical life and finally loses consciousness of them altogether as he passes on to the higher levels of the inner world; but there are many people who have a more serious view of life and who lose no opportunity of acquiring knowledge; and the astral world, which is called "the hall of learning" by students of the occult, furnishes them remarkably good conditions. Here we are limited in three dimensions of matter and hampered by the very narrow range of the physical senses. In the astral world matter has four dimensions and new and marvelous avenues of learning open before the student. Those who are at all interested in music, or art of any kind, find both the field and the facilities enormously extended. Those who study nature, whether by directly probing into her secrets or by cleverly combining her principles into new processes and inventions, have such opportunities as scientist or discoverer has not dreamed of on this plane. And so for all the thoughtful and studious there is a life of the most useful and fascinating kind in the astral world; but it must not be supposed that the avenues to progress are only for the studious. There, as here, the opportunity for useful work in helping humanity forward is boundless; for while poverty and disease have disappeared absolutely there is much philanthropic work of other kinds to be done. There are people to be taught, for there, as here, the majority are sadly in need of knowledge of how to take advantage of nature's laws for our rapid progress, and how to live in harmony with them in order to get the greatest happiness from life; but the work to be done is by no means confined to teaching. The ignorance that makes the teaching so necessary has brought a great many people into the unfortunate condition where immediate assistance is most urgently needed, and there is such a variety of helplessness that nobody need to be idle.

Because of the false teaching upon the subject of life hereafter, many people are bewildered when they become conscious in the astral life. Many have had their minds so vividly impressed with the awful fate that awaits those who are not "saved" before death that they fall into a state of terror when at last they realize that death has really occurred. Those among the so-called dead who are kindly enough to rescue the distressed may come to their relief and give most valuable assistance. Perhaps the commonest thing that engages the attention of the astral worker is the fear that death brings to most people. They arrive in the astral world with the feeling that everything is unknown and uncertain. All preconceived ideas about the life after death have suddenly been found unreliable and they are afraid of they know not what. They want to cling to anybody who knows something of the new world. When we remember that people are arriving in the astral world by the tens of thousands daily, even under normal peace-time conditions, it is evident that all who wish to be of service can find much to do. No special knowledge of the astral plane is necessary, though naturally enough the greater one's knowledge the greater is his usefulness; but common sense is a sufficient equipment in simple work, for those who desire to be useful instead of giving the entire time to the pleasures of that world. The work for the astral helpers ranges upward in complexity, of course, and there is profitable activity for those with the fullest knowledge and skill.

Life on the astral plane has its end for the same reason that it comes to a close on the physical plane. Nature's purpose has been accomplished and the man is ready to go on farther in his evolution. The length of the astral life varies just as it does in the physical world. Some physical lives are very long and sometimes only when five scores of years, or more, have passed does the ego withdraw. Other lives are very short and are scarcely well begun when they unexpectedly come to a close. There is nevertheless a general average to be found. It is at least possible to make averages for different classes of people and to say that a majority of those who are of ordinary health and strength are likely to attain a stated age, while it is certain that the majority of those who have such and such a physical handicap will lose their physical bodies when they are much younger. Such general rules may also be applied to the astral life.

Here a long and alert life is most desirable because the purpose of the physical plane is to gather experience that shall be transmuted into wisdom on a higher plane; but the astral plane is, for the vast majority of the race, related to the purgative process. In that life the errors of the physical existence are largely worked out. The rule of a long life being most desirable on the physical plane is reversed on the astral plane. It is the shortest life in the astral world that is the greatest prize, and it comes to those who have lived the purest and noblest lives while here. The sooner a man gets through the astral world and begins the reaping of his harvest on the mental plane, or heaven world, the better.

The length of the astral sojourn depends primarily upon the durability of the astral body and that, in turn, depends upon the kind of life he has lived here. Let us suppose that he has lived a very gross and sensual life. Let us also imagine that he had an ungovernable temper and frequently gave way to outbursts of fury; further, that he was cruel and revengeful, seeking and finding many opportunities of inflicting injuries upon others. Here we have a case for very long life on the lower levels of the astral world.

Let us now consider a different type of man. He lives peacefully and harmoniously with those about him. He feels strong affection for various people. He has a host of friends because of his cheerful, helpful and sympathetic attitude toward others. He lives cleanly and thinks nobly. His mind is kept free from trivialities and his tongue is never employed in gossip. He makes a determined and persistent effort to eliminate pride, envy and ambition. He cultivates the habit of thinking first of the welfare of others and always last of himself—in short, tries hard to eliminate selfishness and to see all things impersonally. Such a man could know nothing whatever of the disagreeable part of the astral life and would pass quickly through even the higher subdivisions and reach the ecstatic happiness of the heaven world.

From the lower subdivisions the average man rises very gradually to the higher. He remains on a given level for the period that is required to eliminate the matter of that subdivision from his astral body. He is then immediately conscious on the next higher level. The grosser matter falls away because the man has at last stopped sending his life force through it. Ungratified desire has finally worn itself out and he is free. The process can be greatly hastened or retarded by the man's attitude toward life.

If he foolishly dwells upon his desires, he gives new vitality and prolonged life to them. If he can resolutely turn his mind to higher things he hastens his release. His fate is in his own hands, and he is fortunate indeed if he has a knowledge of such matters.

One who dies in advanced years will pass more rapidly through the astral world than he would have done had he died in the full strength of manhood. As the years accumulate, the emotions that vivify the lowest grades of astral matter are not so much in evidence and the matter in which they are expressed loses its vitality. That is an additional reason why it is desirable to live to old age in the physical world.

The hold that the material world has upon the mind is one of the causes which greatly prolong existence in the astral world. Some people give their time and thought so exclusively to material things that after they lose the physical body they cannot keep the mind away from the life that lies behind them. This difficulty does not necessarily arise wholly from having given one's energies entirely to personal ambition and material accumulation. Sometimes the ruler of a country is so determined to still dabble in its affairs, as far as possible, that this vivid interest in the physical world stretches out the period of astral life most unfortunately.

Ordinarily one's sojourn in the astral world is comparatively short, if we measure it in the terms of physical life. A person who has lived here seventy years may have twenty or thirty years on the astral plane. But that will depend not only upon how he lived the physical life just closed but also upon his general position in human evolution. A savage of low type would have a comparatively long astral life while a man at the higher levels of civilization would have a comparatively short period there. The man at somewhat lower levels of civilized life might be said to come in at about midway between the two. But it must be remembered that these are very general estimates and that among civilized peoples individuals differ enormously. Some will pass very slowly and, so far as lower levels are concerned, painfully through astral life, while the sojourn of others is very brief and they pass happily and rapidly from physical death to the heaven world.

Communication with those who have passed on into the astral world is possible, but not always desirable, for a number of reasons. As an evidence of the continuity of consciousness, such communications have been of the greatest service in the hands of the scientific investigator. As a consolation to those who have thus come again in touch with dead friends such messages have been of great value to the bereaved. For a time those who have lost the physical body are usually within easy reach through the usual methods employed for the purpose and perhaps no harm is done by such communications unless they arouse anew the grief of those who have been left behind and thus greatly depress the departed. But when the living dead get farther along, and are much out of touch with the material world, then directing their attention backward may be injurious to them. For that reason careful students of the occult seldom seek to obtain messages, or at least do it with proper consideration for all the circumstances of the particular case.

Due regard for the welfare of those who have passed on, as well as for those who remain, requires that the facts be thoughtfully considered. The truth of the matter is that it is our keen sense of loss that gives rise to the desire for a message of some sort. We long once more to get into touch with one that seems to be lost to us. We are not really thinking much about his welfare. As a matter of fact he has not lost sight of us and does not have our sense of separation. Not only is he able to see us and to be conscious of our feelings and emotions, but during the hours when we are asleep he is in full and free communication with us and we with him. On awakening we usually have no memory of this and if we do we call it a dream. But it is not so with him. His memory of it is perfect and as a consequence he has not our sense of loss.

The result of knowledge upon the subject, which can readily be gained by a study of the researches of the skilled occultists, is that we come to feel that we should rest satisfied with the fact that we do converse with the dead nightly, and leave mediumistic communications to the scientific investigators. The natural order of things is that the person who passes into the astral world shall in time fix his attention exclusively upon the inner life and be completely divorced from physical plane affairs. That is the mental and emotional condition which permits of his rapid passage through levels where he should not linger. It is said that to turn his attention backward at this juncture sometimes causes him acute distress.

A reading of the Christian scriptures with a knowledge of occultism often throws a new light upon the subject. An instance of this is to be found in the story of the woman of Endor who is visited by Saul in his quest for psychic information about the crisis that has been reached in the affairs of his kingdom. The woman went into a trance and acted as a medium for a communication from Samuel, who tells Saul just what will occur in the impending battle. Samuel's first words were a reproach to Saul. "Why hast thou disquieted me to bring me up?"\* was his greeting. It is the language of one who is displeased. Drawing his attention forcibly back to the material world by the strong desire of Saul to communicate with him was evidently distressing, hence the rebuke, "Why hast thou *disquieted* me?"

What is here said on the subject of communication, however, has reference to general principles only. There is no intention of suggesting that it is always undesirable to communicate with those who have passed over. Often those on the other side seek means of communicating and they should find the most willing co-operation from this side. Sometimes one who has left the physical plane life has a message of great importance to deliver and such a case reverses the general rule—he would be delayed if he could *not* communicate. It would be decidedly to his advantage to free his mind of the matter.

---

\* *I Samuel XXVIII—15.*

Until he has done so he may remain in a restless condition and his case falls into the category of what the spiritualists call "earth bound." He may have left undone something that a message will set right, if he can get it through, or he may have secreted something that cannot be found because he died suddenly and had no opportunity to speak of it; or it may simply be a case of desiring to prove to materialistic friends the fact that the so-called dead are not dead, and are close at hand. It is sometimes possible for the important information to come through into physical life in the form of a dream by the living, and thus the recovery of valuables has followed.*

It sometimes happens that one who thus earnestly desires to communicate but is wholly ignorant of how to accomplish his purpose causes a great deal of annoyance. His blundering attempts to use psychic force may be wholly abortive and result in meaningless noises, raps, the tumbling of books or dishes from shelves or the aimless movements of furniture. Annoyance may sometimes be caused also by intention, on the part of those who think it is humorous to play pranks. It must be remembered that passing on to the astral life does not improve one's common sense. If while living here, he thought it amusing to astonish or delude somebody, or trick a friend into seriously accepting some absurd assertion as a fact, he still regards the same course as entertain-

---

\* See *Dreams*, by Leadbeater, and *Dreams and Premonitions*, by Rogers.

ing. This accounts for many of the foolish and sometimes startling messages, or answers to questions, received at seances.

It has often been asked why, if communication between the physical and astral planes is possible, we do not receive information that might lead to valuable discoveries and inventions. The very fact that death does not confer wisdom explains it in part. But an even more important fact is that communication is easier with the lower levels and correspondingly difficult as the higher levels are reached. All who have had much experience with seances are familiar with the fact that the majority of the messages are commonplace. Most of the inhabitants of the astral levels with which communication is easy are not the type capable of furnishing ideas of any great value. It is on the higher levels that the man of intellectual power passes most of his astral life. The scientist or the inventor who has given so much thought to his work that he has been in some degree successful here is likely to pass swiftly through lower levels. It is the highest of the seven subdivisions of the astral world that is the habitat of the person who has followed intellectual pursuits during physical life, and with that level it is practically impossible for the ordinary medium to communicate.

One of the objections to indiscriminate communication with the astral plane lies in the fact that the lowest class of entities are most accessible. That not only accounts for the commonplace messages in such abundance, but it is frequently a source of actual danger, especially where people form "circles" for the purpose of rendering themselves more sensitive to psychic influences. In such cases it is common to accept every message as absolute truth. There is no doubt that as a rule the astral people who manage such a gathering are earnest and honest; but they are neither all-wise nor all-powerful, and it sometimes comes about that some of the sitters are partially or wholly obsessed by astral entities, and should that occur it might prove to be an exceedingly serious matter.

Probably there is no astral subject of more vital importance to any of us than that of the right attitude of mind and emotion toward the living dead. It is commonly said that we can do nothing more for them when they have passed away from physical plane life, but a greater error could not easily be made. The connection with us is by no means severed. Not only are they emotionally in touch with us but their emotions are very much keener than when they had a physical body through which to express them. They are now living in the astral body, the matter of which is enormously more responsive to emotional vibrations. A joyous emotion here would be tremendously more joyous there and a thing that would produce depression would be enormously more depressing there. That fact should give pause to those who are inclined to think in sorrow, and with something of despair, of their friends who have passed on. They are not far away in space and our strong emotions affect them profoundly.

We are all familiar with the fact that moods are

communicable. The person who is cheerful cheers up others in his vicinity, while the one who is gloomy spreads gloom wherever he goes. It is a simple matter of vibrations. It is often within the power of a member of the family who habitually has "the blues" to destroy the happiness of the entire household. If we think of the most depressing effect that can be caused by sorrow on the physical plane, and then multiply its effectiveness many times we shall have no exaggeration of the astral results of the emotions we indulge in the physical body. If, then, the sorrow of a weeping relative distresses us here it is clear that it must bring really keen distress to the one who is the subject of such grief. His life may thus be made miserable by the very persons who would be the last to cause him sorrow if they understood what they were doing.

We can really help the so-called dead and make them very much happier simply by changing our mournful attitude toward them. All violent expressions of grief should be avoided and a determination to make the best of the matter should be cultivated. The situation may indeed be bad, but we make it very much worse by our mourning. The funeral customs of Occidental civilization are quite consistent with its materialism. We act as nearly as possible as though we believe the dead are lost to us forever.

A more sensible attitude of mind may be observed at any theosophical funeral and, with growing frequency, at the funerals among all thinking people. A funeral should not be the occasion of a final expression of grief, but a gathering of friends who send kindly thoughts and helpful good wishes to the comrade whose life work in the physical world is finished. The general feeling should be very much like that of a party of friends who go to the pier to see a well loved traveler off on a long journey to remote parts of the earth for a sojourn of many years or possibly a lifetime. There should be constant thought of his welfare, not of the loss to his friends. Grief that thinks of itself is an expression of selfishness and is detrimental to all. One should practice self-control in such matters just as one would control the emotion of anger under different circumstances.

Naturally enough the control of grief, when one we love has passed on, is none too easy. But any degree of success is much better than no effort, and will certainly help the one for whom we mourn. Much can be accomplished by avoiding unnecessary incidents that vividly bring back the keen sense of loss. Many people indulge the custom of regularly visiting the cemetery where the body has been interred. A little analysis will show that this is only another evidence of our materialistic modes of thought, and the custom serves to perpetuate gloomy emotions that should never have existed. We cannot, of course, think too often nor too tenderly of those who have passed on, but we should do nothing that leads us to think of them as being dead, or being far away. The fact that they are alive and well and happy and near should constantly fill the mind; and all of that, in nearly all cases, will be perfectly true

## The Astral Life

if we do not foolishly destroy their peace of mind with our selfish sorrow.

Occasionally a hint on the subject comes from the astral plane people themselves. In a book* by Sir Oliver Lodge on his experiments in psychic research, there is a message from his son, who was killed in battle, agreeing to attend the family Christmas dinner and to occupy the chair placed for him, provided they will all refrain from gloomy thoughts about him! No one who is informed on the subject of emotional reaction on the astral body, after the loss of the physical body, could be surprised by the conditions named by the young man.

The advocates of cremation have a strong argument in the fact that the preservation of the body for a time, whether in a tomb or a grave, tends to keep grief alive. When the body is reduced to ashes the delusion that the body is somehow the man seems to have less of a material basis. Visits to a tomb or grave are unfortunate, not alone because they renew grief through thinking upon it and thus cause great distress to those for whom we mourn, but also because the environment of a cemetery is one of the worst possible for the sorrowing. It is a dismal park of concentrated griefs where each mourner accentuates the emotional distress of all others. There is but one sensible attitude to take toward those who have passed on—to think of them as living a joyous, busy life and probably calling on us daily even though most of us are not sensitive

---

* *Raymond: or Life and Death.*—Lodge.

enough to be conscious of the fact. We should try to realize the truth of the matter and then readjust our habits to fit the facts. The average person who is afflicted with the erroneous ideas still so common, is doing an enormous amount of injury and is bringing into the lives of the very people he loves a depression of which he little dreams, and which he can change to vivid pleasure by always thinking cheerfully of them and sending them daily thoughts of peace and serenity.

## CHAPTER IX.

## REBIRTH: ITS REASONABLENESS

The soundest ground upon which anything can rest is its inherent reasonableness. From that viewpoint, let us examine the idea that the multitudes of people about us are old souls in new bodies. Perhaps the greatest folly of which one can be guilty is to reject an idea instantly because it is wholly different from what he has previously believed. That limits him to his present idea, whatever it may be, and quite regardless of how erroneous it may be. If people were not willing to examine unaccustomed ideas, the world would make no progress. If that had always been the attitude of everybody in the past, if they had clung tenaciously to the ideas with which they were born, we should still believe that the earth is flat and that slavery is a necessary human institution. In short, if we did not seriously examine what often appears at first statement to be almost impossible, and perhaps absurd, all the follies and superstitions of the past would still be afflicting mankind.

Let us consider the human infant as we see it at birth. Whence came it? How can we account for it in a universe of law? We can understand it from the material side. Its tiny body is a concourse of physical atoms with a prenatal history of a few months. But its mind, its consciousness, its emotions, what of them? The average man replies that God made them and they constitute the soul. But how and when were they "made"? Even the material part of this infant did not spring miraculously and instantaneously into existence. How much less possible it is that the soul did so! If we say "God made it" we have explained nothing. The process of its creation was evolutionary. Nobody denies that the earth was created by evolution, although men may differ in opinion on the matter of a divine intelligence guiding its evolutionary development. The same truth must apply to the human intelligence.

Lodge wrote *Life and Matter* as a reply to Haeckel's *Riddle of the Universe,* which presented the latter's philosophy of materialism. But Lodge did more than demolish Haeckel's premise and leave him with not an inch of scientific ground to support his theory. The English scientist raised questions that have not been answered, and cannot be answered, by the materialist. He points out that the materialist's philosophy has no explanation for "the extraordinary rapidity of development which results in the production of a fully endowed individual in the course of some fraction of a century."*

With those two dozen words Lodge leaves the scientific materialist speechless; for scientists are evolutionists, and it is impossible to account for *"the extraordinary rapidity of development"* by the laws of evolution. It is well known that evolutionary age

---

* *Life and Matter.*—Lodge, p. 121.

is indicated by complexity. A simple form is comparatively young while a complex one has a long evolutionary history behind it. The earth is simple compared to a human being. If, then, it has required ages to evolve the earth to its present stage how long did it take to evolve the wonderfuly complex mental and emotional nature of the human being that inhabits the earth? And thus Lodge bottles Haeckel up on his own premises and shows that the evolutionary principles to which the naturalist appeals demolish his theory! He practically says to Haeckel, "Your philosophy, sir, fails to show how it is possible for the vacuous mind of the infant to evolve into the genius of the philosopher in thirty or forty years." In other words, if the infant is nothing but the form we see it would be utter absurdity to say that that mass of matter can evolve a high grade of intelligence within a few years when it takes centuries to make a slight evolutionary gain.

Look at an infant the day it is born. Study its face. One might as well search the surface of a squash for some indication of intelligence. But wait only a little while and you shall have evidence not merely of intelligence but of emotions possible only to the highest order of life. Clearly, here is something not evolved within a brief period from a mass of material atoms. Such a theory would be as unscientific as the popular belief in miraculous creation at which the scientific materialist scoffs. The swift change from the vacuity of the infant mind to the intellectual power of the adult in the "fraction of a century" is not the creation of something but its *manifestation—the coming through into visible expression of that which already exists.* The soul, the consciousness, the real man, consisting of the whole of the mental and emotional nature, which has been built up through thousands of years of evolution, is coming once more to rebirth, to visible expression in a material body.

The body is, of course, but the new physical instrument of the old soul—an instrument, as certainly as the violin is an instrument and a vehicle for the musician's expression. At every turn our materialistic conceptions mislead us and prevent the perception of nature's truth. It is because we think of the body as being actually the person, that it seems improbable that an old soul has entered the infant body. We think of the power and intelligence of an old soul and then look at the baby and find no indication of such things. But that is only because the baby body is such a new and undeveloped instrument that it is at first useless and only slowly can it be brought under control of the soul and made to express its intelligence and power. The body is a growing instrument, not a completed one.

Let us suppose that musical instruments grow as physical bodies do. Suppose there was a time when the piano was keyless. Suppose that sounding boards have a period of immaturity and that the whole mechanism of the instrument is in a state that can only be characterized as infantile. If a master musician attempts to play on such a piano his performance would by no means be an indication of his ability. A competent critic who could hear the performance but not see the musician would promptly declare that no really great musician was touching the keys. And that is precisely the mistake we make in assuming that the immature body of an infant is capable of expressing the intellectual power of the old soul, or, to put it differently, denying that a returned old soul is in possession of the infant body simply because there is no physical plane evidence of the fact. If pianos slowly grew to maturity then only when the instrument was mature could the master musician give a practical demonstration of his skill; and only when the physical body has reached its maturity can the soul that is using it fully express itself.

In the early years of the physical body the soul is only very partially expressed through it. The entrance of the consciousness into the physical world is slow and gradual. Beginning some months before the birth of the physical body and continuing for a period of several years the soul, or consciousness, is engaged in the process of anchoring itself in the physical world. For a long time the center of consciousness remains above the material plane and during the early years of childhood the consciousness is divided between the astral and physical worlds, with the result that the child is often somewhat confused and brings fragments of astral consciousness into physical life. When the physical body is about seven years old the consciousness may be said to be centered on the physical plane, but only when the body and brain of the soul's new instrument are mature has the opportunity come for the fullest expression.

Some of the difficulties commonly associated in the mind with the thought of the pre-existence and rebirth of the soul will disappear if we do not lose sight of the fact that the soul is a center of consciousness, which is always conscious somewhere, but which very gradually shifts its focus from plane to plane. Its permanent home is in that body of subtle matter drawn about the ego in the higher levels of the heaven world. From that point it sends energies outward and draws about itself in the lower levels of the mental world a body, or vehicle of consciousness, that is *not* permanent but which will serve the purpose of functioning for a period on that plane. Downward or outward again the energies are sent, building about the center of consciousness on the astral plane a temporary body of astral matter, temporary in the same sense that the physical body is temporary, and which shall serve the consciousness in the astral, or emotional world, during the whole of the physical plane life and for some time afterward. Still outward, or downward, the soul sends its energies till the material world is reached, when it begins to function partially, and very feebly, through the infant physical body.

That we learn by experience, nobody will deny. That the events of daily life develop intellect and compassion is too obvious for argument; but it is equally clear that the mental and moral difference between the savage state and the civilized life is so great that only a very small portion of the evolutionary work can be done in the longest physical existence possible to man. The way in which nature accomplishes so great an achievement is by repeated visits of the soul to the physical realm. During the interval between physical lives the consciousness abides on its own plane in the spiritual world. The thought is turned inward instead of outward. That state of consciousness, being greater than this one, includes a memory of the physical life just closed. The soul during that period may be likened to a man who, at the close of a busy day, retreats to the privacy of his fireside and there goes thoughtfully over the day's events. He seeks out of memory's record all the blunders he has made and by careful analysis fortifies himself against a repetition of such mistakes in the future. As he reviews the record, he sees with satisfaction the good points it contains and he resolves to be even more helpful to others on the morrow. He outlines in his mind the affairs of the next day and determines to make the most of his opportunities. The result of all this is that he will begin the active life again on the following morning, not only rested and refreshed for the day's program but at a somewhat advanced mental and moral level. He starts wiser and stronger than he was on the previous day. And even so it is with the soul, the real man. The centuries of blissful life that elapse before the return here, give opportunity for the complete digestion and assimilation of all the experiences, great and small, of the period that closed with the death of the physical body. On its next visit to the physical plane the soul will begin at a higher point in its evolution than in the previous life, because the period of assimilation will have transmuted past experience into wisdom and a better brain will express that wisdom in the following incarnation.

The soul is the life, the thought, the emotions, the intelligence. Everything about the human being that is not material belongs to the soul side, the life side. All that is physical constitutes the environment of the soul. The physical body is as much a part of the soul's environment as a house is. The soul comes and goes. It appears, disappears and reappears in the visible world, and each time it lives in a new body. That body is its temporary house. Imagine a naturalist journeying to far lands where the climatic conditions permit but a short stay and where only a rude shelter can be erected. Each year he comes to gather specimens. He constructs a temporary house, accumulates his store of material, and then retires with it to his permanent home in a more genial clime. There at his leisure, under the most favorable conditions, he classifies the specimens, studies them profoundly and adds another harvest of wisdom to the lessons he learned on preceding journeys.

Even so does the soul come, seeking in the rude material world the experience that will give it greater wisdom. It also lives in a temporary house, called a body, that time will destroy. That body serves the same purpose for the soul that the temporary hut does for the naturalist. Like the naturalist, the soul retires with its accumulations to a more genial clime, the heaven world, and there it also deeply studies its sentient experiences, gleaning from them another harvest of wisdom to add to its spiritual wealth.

In trying to understand the relationship of the soul to the universe it should never be forgotten that the permanent residence of the soul is on the inner planes and that a lifetime here is, comparatively, but a fleeting visit. In the case of the naturalist, when the season suitable for his brief sojourn in the far country arrives, he turns his attention to it and roughly outlines in his thought the work he will do. Then he takes the necessary steps to bring his consciousness into contact with the work—that is, he travels to the scene of his coming activities. Analogous to that is the task of the soul, which is the real man. Having finished the assimilation of the experiences obtained in the previous embodiment he again turns his energies outward toward the material plane. As it would be impossible for the naturalist to accomplish his purpose at a distance, so it is for the soul. In each case the consciousness must be brought to function where the work is to be done. There must be a means of approach. The naturalist cannot see and hear and collect at a distance. No more can a soul receive vibrations from the material world. To get experience here it must be encased in a physical body. The naturalist brings his consciousness into contact with the work by the media of railways and ships. The soul accomplishes the task by drawing about itself an instrument composed of the next lower grade of matter and we call that instrument its mental body. Sending its consciousness outward through that it is able to come into contact with astral matter, and to fashion another vehicle from that. Through the astral matter it can contact physical matter and express itself in the material world. If, with clairvoyant sight, we could observe the true, the inner man, we should perceive the subtle bodies through which alone he can be conscious here —the physical body surrounded and permeated by the matter of the astral body, then both the physical and astral bodies enveloped and interpenetrated by the matter of the mental body, and all three of them within the embracing control of the causal, or spiritual body. All these together constitute the mechanism through which the soul sends its energies outward into expression in less spiritual realms; and through them alone can it become conscious of the material plane. Now, there is a most important distinction between some of these visible and invisible bodies, or vehicles of consciousness, and it is that the causal, or spiritual, vehicle is the only one that does not perish before another incarnation begins. The physical, astral and mental bodies are but temporary aggregations of matter that the soul uses for a while and then discards. Not so the causal body. It persists and plays a wonderful part in the soul's evolution. It is composed of matter that is very little like matter as we know it. Perhaps we may call it spiritual matter, but matter that is so much nearer to the source of being that it scintillates with the essence of life. This spiritual body may be called the permanent residence of the soul, during the period of human evolution, from which its energies are sent outward through the mental and astral into the physical body. It is also a hall of records, for in it is, in epitome, the result of past experiences gathered through all the incarnations. To liken it to a phonograph record that can both record and reproduce words, would not be a perfect simile, but it is at least a suggestion. If a phonograph could not only record all that is said in its vicinity but all that is thought and felt and seen, and was itself a living thing that could then take the whole of those experiences, extract and absorb the mental and moral lessons they teach, and could put those lessons at its own service in such a readjustment of its mechanism as would enable it in the future to exclude the trivial and record only the valuable for its more rapid evolution, it would then do for an analogy of at least a part of the functions of the causal body.

One great purpose served by the causal body is the conservation of energy. While the mental, astral and physical bodies perish in each incarnation, the persisting spiritual body has recorded and preserved the gist of all the experiences they enabled the soul to get. Therefore all the skill and knowledge evolved has been stored in the causal body and can be used in following incarnations in the exact degree that the new lower vehicles are able to transmit its lofty vibrations. That is one reason why it is so important to purify the lower bodies and make them responsive. It is because what we learn in each life is preserved in each individual that the progress of the race is possible. Each old soul brings back and expresses through the new physical body the accumulated harvests of past lives.

For the time being the soul's evolution lies on the physical plane where certain lessons are to be learned. After the early years of childhood are over the consciousness is firmly anchored here, where the chief work is to be done, during the hours of the waking life. During sleep the ego temporarily abandons the physical body and functions in the astral body in the astral world. The material body sleeping here is merely a deserted and empty vehicle, magnetically connected with the soul, awaiting its return.

As childhood, youth, maturity, and old age pass, complex experiences come to the soul thus functioning here. Other souls functioning through physical bodies are encountered and various relationships are established. Out of the complexity of social, business, religious, and political activities the soul gets a large and varied experience. Sooner or later the death of the physical body closes the chapter. The gathering of such experiences has ceased, not because the soul has acquired all possible physical world knowledge, but because its instrument of consciousness here has worn out and ceased to function.

Death cuts the soul off from its physical plane connection and the center of its consciousness is then shifted to the astral plane. There the purgative process goes forward, as previously explained. As that proceeds the soul gradually gets free from one grade of astral matter after another and with the disappearance of each the man becomes conscious

## Rebirth: Its Reasonableness

on a higher level. The physical body is lost in a moment but the matter of the astral body gradually wears away until there is so little left that the soul has lost connection with the astral world also. This means that the center of consciousness has shifted to the mental plane, or heaven world, where the man will live until his next incarnation.

There in the mental world, functioning through the vehicle of mental matter, a very important process goes on. The heaven world life is a harvest time in which assimilation of experience takes place. The consciousness there deeply broods over the experiences of the physical life and extracts the essence from them which is transmuted into faculty and power for future greater expression. It is thus that the soul grows in wisdom and power through its long evolution.

When the heaven life is finished, when experience has been transmuted and the net gain has been built into the enduring causal body, the mental body, like the astral, has been dissipated. The end of the cycle has come and the physical, astral and mental bodies have all perished. Nothing remains but the soul, the real man, functioning through the causal body, which persists. From that the ego again sends the forces outward, in the first activity toward rebirth, forming a new mental body by drawing about itself the matter of the lower levels of the mental plane, then securing a new astral body on the astral plane and finally taking possession of another infant body in process of formation on the physical plane, into which it will in due course be reborn.

Another incarnation has begun. Again the soul will have the experiences of childhood, youth, maturity, and old age. In the early part of the incarnation it slowly secures fuller and firmer possession of its new physical instrument—the material body—and passes through a period of recapitulation.

We must not lose sight of the fact that during the stay on inner planes the soul has progressed in evolution and has returned with greater mental capacity and deeper moral insight than it has ever before possessed. It is now capable of acquiring new and more difficult lessons than it could have mastered in its previous incarnation. Thus each incarnation marks an advance in the long evolutionary journey. In each physical life it develops something of intellect and strengthens somewhat the moral nature. The objective is to bring them both into their highest possible expression. When, after a long series of incarnations, this is accomplished, the individual becomes a combination of saint and genius and passes on to superphysical and superhuman evolutions to return no more, unless in a voluntary incarnation as one of the teachers and saviours of the human race.

The period between these consecutive appearances of the soul in a succession of physical bodies varies greatly and depends on a number of things. The length of time spent upon the astral plane has already been discussed. The time spent in the heaven world depends upon the mental and moral forces generated during the physical and astral life. If there is a great harvest of experience it will require a longer time to transmute it, while, of course, one who has thought little and loved but little will have a shorter period there, for it is the emotional and intellectual activities that have their culmination in the mental world. The subject is a rather complex one and other factors come into play, including the intensity of the heaven world life. In general terms, however, it can be said that the heaven life of the ordinarily intelligent person will commonly be a period several times the length of his combined physical and astral life. Some people will have only two or three hundred years between incarnations while others may have six or seven centuries and still others a much longer period.

In getting a right understanding of the subject of rebirth, or reincarnation, it is necessary to keep in mind the fact that the soul, or center of individualized consciousness, is the man and that the physical body is merely an instrument he uses for a number of years; that the causal body is his permanent body for the whole of human evolution; that the higher mental plane is his home plane and that from there he sends forth successive expressions of himself into these lower regions. With such facts before us there should be no confusion of thought about the successive personalities of an individual; yet we sometimes hear people speak of the absurdity of supposing that a person can be one man in one incarnation and another man at a later rebirth. Of course no such thing occurs. An individual remains the same individual forever. "But," objects the critic, "may I not have been Mr. Smith in England a few hundred years ago, whereas I am now certainly Mr. Brown, in America? If so is that not a case of being two individuals?"

It is not a case of being two individuals. It is a case of one individual being expressed through a physical body a few hundred years ago in England, dying from it, spending a fairly long period in the astral plane and heaven world, and then again expressing himself through another physical body in America at the present time. The confusion of thought on the part of the questioner arises from thinking of the physical body as being the man; but it is no more the man than the clothing he wears. It is true that he is known at one period as Smith and at another as Brown, but that no more affects his individuality than the assumption of an *alias* by a fleeing criminal changes him. The name applies exclusively to the physical body, or personality, as distinguished from the individuality. That body is but the temporary clothing of the soul. Let us suppose that a man's name were applied to his clothing and changed with his clothing as it does with his body. We might then know him as Mr. Lightclothes in the summer and Mr. Darkclothes in the winter, but neither the change of clothing or name would make him somebody else. The majority of women change their names in each incarnation. A man may know a certain woman as Miss Smith when she is a slip of a girl, free from care and with little serious thought of life. Twenty years later she may be Mrs. Brown, his wife, a thoughtful matron, the mother of children. She has changed her name and greatly changed in character, too, but she is the same individual.

It seems possible that a person may change as much between infancy and old age as between this incarnation and the next. Even the difference between a youth of twenty years who is an artist and the same man at three score and ten who has given forty years to scientific study and research, may be enormous, but the individuality is, of course, identical. He has rapidly evolved and greatly improved, and that is just what occurs to the soul by repeated rebirths—steady evolutionary development of the permanent individual.

The reincarnating process by which the soul evolves is somewhat analogous to the growth of a young physical body. The process consists of alternating periods of objective and subjective activity. How does the body of a child grow? It consumes food, the objective activity. It then digests and assimilates it, the subjective procedure. These periods must alternate or there can be no growth, because neither alone is the complete process. The one is the complement of the other. So it is in the evolution of the soul by reincarnation. The experience of life is the food on which the soul grows. The physical plane existence is the objective period in which the food is gathered. At death the man passes into the invisible realms where the subjective process is carried on. He digests and assimilates his experiences and the gist of these experiences is stored in the causal body. What food is to the growth of the physical body, experience is to the growth of the spiritual body.

The same law governs mental and moral growth, as it operates in our daily affairs. A young man is in college. How does his intellect develop? By precisely the same process of alternating periods of objective and subjective activity. In the classroom the instructor puts a mathematical problem on the blackboard and explains it. With the outward senses of sight and hearing, aided by pencil and notebook, the student gathers the food for mental growth. This period of objective activity comes to an end and he then retires to the privacy of his room and there the subjective period begins. He deeply thinks over the problem. His material, the food for mental growth, is only a few notes that serve to keep the problem in his mind. At first all that they signify is not obvious, but as he turns the various points over and over in his mind their significance becomes clearer and fuller. It is the subjective process of digestion. Little by little new light dawns in the student's mind. Finally he has complete comprehension of the mathematical principles involved, and the process of assimilation is finished. This subjective period is the complement of the objective period and they must go on alternating or intellectual growth will stop. When the process of digestion and assimilation is finished the student must return to the classroom for further mental food and when he arrives it is by virtue of the fact that he did digest the previous lesson that he is able to take a higher and more difficult one. Precisely so it is with the reincarnating soul. In the interval between incarnations it so assimilates the experiences of the last physical life that it comes to rebirth with added abilities which enable it to take higher and more difficult lessons than it could previously master.

In the case of both physical growth by eating and mental growth by instruction there is no possible escape from the law of alternating periods of objective and subjective activity. When the child has digested and assimilated a meal there is but one possible thing that can follow—return to his source of supply for another meal. When the student has digested and assimilated the lesson given to him the only possibility of further mental growth lies in his return to the classroom for more material. And so it is with the human soul in its work of evolving its latent powers and possibilities. There is no other road forward but the cyclic one that brings it back to the physical life incarnation after incarnation, but at a higher point than it previously touched. The hunger of the child that insures its return to the table for more food is analogous to the desire of the soul for sentient expression that brings it to rebirth.

These alternating periods are found everywhere in the economy of nature. All her evolutionary expressions are cyclic. But the cyclic movement is not in closed circles. It represents a spiral. The "evolutionary ladder" that the soul climbs is a winding stairway. In its upward progress it makes many rounds but it is always ascending and never returns to the same point. In each cycle, that is made up of the journey from the heaven world through the astral plane, into the physical and then back through the astral plane into the heaven world, it touches each of them at a higher point, or in a higher state of development, than it had previously attained. Each rebirth finds it abler to gather a larger harvest of experience here and each return to the mental plane, or heaven world, finds it abler to digest and assimilate its experiences and to comprehend more of the realities of the life of its home plane.

This round, or cycle, through the physical, astral, and mental regions, is a continuous progressive journey of the soul which began away back at the dawn of mind in man and will continue until he is the perfected mental and moral being. In each incarnation here he gathers experience in proportion to his alertness and to the opportunities his previous lives have made for him. He learns to help others, to be sympathetic, to be tolerant. Such activities will give him pleasure in the astral life and joy and wisdom in the mental region, or heaven world. But he also does some evil things. He makes enemies, he generates hatred and he injures others. This will give him distress in the astral life and no results for soul growth or general progress in the heaven world. If he does an equal amount of good and harm his progress will be slow. If he does much good and little evil his progress will be rapid and his existence happy. If he is a man of great energy, and no very great moral development, and selfishly does much harm, he will suffer much in the astral life.

It often puzzles the student of elementary Theosophy to be told that the soul passes through the

# Rebirth: Its Reasonableness

purgation of the astral plane and goes on into the heaven world only to return to another incarnation and later to enter the astral purgatory again. Why, it is asked, must one who has thus been purified be again purified?

The astral reactions are the results of the blunders made in each lifetime. Each of us in any given incarnation creates by his wrongdoing the only purgatory that awaits him after death. If he does no wrong there cannot possibly be any painful reaction. As a matter of occult fact the average good man will find the astral plane life a happy existence and will soon pass on to the blissful heaven world. As for the evil doer the suffering relates only to his evil deeds. Let us assume that he has committed murder. When the reaction of the evil force he has generated is over and he passes on into the heaven plane it does not mean that he is incapable of future evil. It means that he has probably learned thoroughly the lesson that it is very foolish to take life. But there are many other lessons he has not learned. When he passes into the heaven world he temporarily leaves all evil behind him. He is as one who puts his shoes aside to enter a temple. The astral body, like the physical, has perished and it is the freed soul that enters the heaven world. But when he returns through the astral plane to reincarnation he is clothed again in astral matter and this new astral body is exactly representative of his attainments in evolution. In his coming incarnation he will have other physical plane experiences and learn other lessons. The next time probably he will not kill, but perhaps he will cheat and steal or be a drunkard. These errors will react upon him in the astral life that follows. In a coming incarnation he will be wise enough to be temperate and neither cheat nor steal; but perhaps he will be a gossip and work much evil through slander. This in turn will bring its pain; and so in time he will learn to generate no evil force at all but to live in good will and helpfulness toward everybody. Then his progress will be rapid indeed, his life on all planes will be happy and the painful part of human evolution will, for him, be over.

The purpose of evolution is no less obvious than the fact of evolution. Evolution is an unfolding process in which the simple becomes the complex and the inner life is more and more fully expressed in the outer form. The development and improvement in form keeps pace with the necessities of the unfolding life. In the lowest levels in the animal kingdom the form is but a cell. But as the life comes into fuller and fuller expression, limbs for locomotion, and in due course, the organs for hearing and seeing, and the other mechanism of the developing consciousness, are evolved. In the human kingdom the vehicle of consciousness comes to its highest possible form and then evolution goes on in the perfecting of that physical form. In the process of continually changing the matter of the body it is possible for the brain to be constantly improved and the whole body to grow more and more sensitive and gradually to become a better and truer expression of the evolving life within. In each incarnation the physical body thus improves. The evolution of life and form necessarily go forward together. Ultimately perfection of form, as well as perfection of intellect and morality, will be reached and human evolution will be finished.

The purpose of evolution, then, is clear. Man is a god in the making—not actually, but only potentially a god, a being to whom all wisdom, perfect compassion and unlimited power are possible; and by the process of evolution he changes the latent into the active. He is at first only an individualized center of consciousness within the All-Consciousness, a mere fragment of the divine life. His relationship to the Supreme Being is something like that of a seed to its plant, a product of it that has latent within it all the characteristics of the plant and the power to become a plant. It is not a plant and neither is man a god; but when the seed has sent out a sprout and taken root in the soil it is a plant in the making; and when the human being has begun to evolve the latent spiritual qualities he is a god in the making. The theosophical view is that man is essentially divine.

Critics sometimes ask why, if man is originally divine, it is necessary for him to pass through any evolutionary process. Divinity indicates merely the essential nature of the human being, not his possession of either knowledge or power or any degree of spiritual perfection. It is as though we should say that the infant son of a great king is royal. The word "royal," like the word "divine," indicates a relationship. The baby royalist is not a king; but he is a king in the making. He has much to learn. He must be educated in statecraft and he must acquire the art of diplomacy. After much experience he will, in time, be capable of ruling an empire. At present this helpless infant bears little resemblance to a king. Nevertheless, on the day of his birth he was as royal as his father. In the same sense the divinity of man represents potential possibilities rather than an obvious fact of the moment. Man is an embryo god and, in time, he shall evolve faculties and powers that his present limited consciousness can not even comprehend. He is not an ephemeral creature of physical origin that lives a brief span to catch a glimpse of immortality and perish, but a spark of the divine life that shall evolve into flame.

Some people accept evolution as a matter of course, in a general way, but they appear unwilling to admit that the race has really made any evolutionary progress. They doubt whether the world is growing better. They feel that the race is just as wicked today as at any time within recorded history. It is true that things are still bad enough but they are certainly enormously better than they were some centuries ago. To say that the world is full of crime and violence proves nothing; nor does even the fact that a civilized nation reverts to the wartime practices of savage life furnish real ground for a pessimistic view. What we have to do in determining whether there has been any racial progress in morality is to take as our standard of measurement something that tests the collective conscience. How does the world of today view war and how did the world in the day of Caesar regard it? There is plenty to shock us now but the very fact that it does shock us is the best evidence of moral progress. Atrocities were expected and taken as a matter of course some centuries ago. They are not the rule now but the rare exception and those guilty of them are likely to make their name a byword among nations. Well within the era of recorded history the usages of nations condemned prisoners of war to become slaves for life. Now the rule is to feed and clothe them and at the end of the conflict send them home.

A simple thing like public sports may be used as a test of public morals. They show what the collective conscience approves. In these days there is very little of brutality in public sports. In some countries bull fighting still lingers; but if we look backward to the Roman period we find a cruelty in public sports that is comparatively shocking. According to the historians, gladiators were compelled to fight to the death. Offenders were devoured by starving wild beasts, and it all made a Roman holiday. Such "sports" would, of course, be utterly impossible anywhere in the world today; but at that time they were matters of course in the life of the world's greatest empire. The fact that the race has evolved morally and that the collective conscience marks a higher point on the ethical thermometer than in the past is too obvious for argument.

How are we to account for that evolutionary progress? It will not do to say that the Christian religion has wrought the change because, splendid as are the teachings of the Christ, the world at large has not accepted them and shaped its civilization by them. If it had done so, a world war would have been impossible. Not only have the so-called Christian nations wrangled and fought over commercial spoils through all their history but class has been arrayed against class and the gain in either personal liberty or economic improvement has been wrested by force from those who profited by the misfortunes of others. In other words, the particular improvements that should have been brought about by religion were compelled, not freely volunteered. Religious teaching helps but, allowing all we reasonably may for the influence of Christianity, we are still unable to account for the change in the common conscience of the race, an evolutionary gain that has been going on steadily since long, long before the coming of Christ—gradual improvement that is by no means confined to Christian nations. It is as pronounced in Asia as in Europe. How then shall we account for it?

If the hypothesis of reincarnation is sound the progress of the race in morality becomes simple. The majority of the great groups of souls that constituted the civilized nations in the time when Rome was the monarch of the Occidental world have had several incarnations since, and in each sojourn on the astral plane have had the severe lesson of the painful reaction from cruelty to others. Thus does nature gradually change the cruel man into the merciful man. In every incarnation the soul grows more humane as well as more intelligent. All of the lessons learned in any incarnation are carried forward into the next life, and thus compassion grows until there is ultimately perfect sympathy with all suffering. Both the progress of the soul and of the race are comprehensible from the viewpoint of reincarnation.

Except by that hypothesis how is it possible to explain such evolutionary progress? Those who do not believe in the pre-existence of the soul and hold that it is in some way brought into being at birth, are put in the very illogical position of saying that the reason why the world is better now than it was in the Roman period is because it pleases God to create a better kind of souls now than He created then!

The principle of rebirth holds also with the animal kingdom at a high level in it. The last phase of evolution in the animal kingdom is the individualizing of the consciousness. A particularly intelligent cat or dog, for example, may be just finishing animal evolution and will be reborn at a low human level. Previous to its individualization it evolves in a group with others of its kind, animated by a common ensoulment that has not reached the level of complete self-consciousness. At that group-soul stage the experience of each animal in the group adds to the knowledge of all. This theosophical teaching on one of nature's most interesting facts enables us to understand many things that would otherwise remain baffling. Instinct has never been satisfactorily explained. Some of its best known expressions are altogether mysterious. Why does a young wild animal hide from the enemies of its kind but not from friends, when it has never seen either? A quail a day old will fall upon its side with a chip or clod firmly clutched in its tiny claws to hide its body, and remain perfectly motionless at the approach of a human being, but will take no alarm at the passing of a squirrel or a rabbit. Why, in remote places like the antarctic regions, are both young and old birds and animals unafraid of man? The group-soul is a clear and simple explanation of all such phenomena. The youngest have the knowledge of the oldest because they are attached to the same group-soul, or source of consciousness. The young quail of this season come back to rebirth from the group-soul that is the storehouse of the experiences of the quail that were killed by men in past seasons, and thus all young things know the common enemy. In the remote regions referred to the killing proclivities of the human being have not become known and there is no "instinct" to warn.

An interesting bit of evidence on the subject of the group-soul is the fact, often chronicled but not explained, that when telephone lines are built in new countries the birds fly against the wires and are killed by thousands, the first season; but when the next season's birds are hatched they are wise and avoid the wires! If the group-soul were not a fact it would naturally require a long time for wire education. No such sudden adjustment would be possible.

Reincarnation represents continuous evolution with no waste of time or loss of energy. Death is not the sudden break in the life program that the popular belief pictures it. The common view of death is as erroneous as the common view of birth. If death were really what most people believe it to be it would constitute a blunder of nature—an irrational interruption of orderly development. In nature's economy there is conservation of energy and no loss can arise through the change called death. If the popular belief that at death we go far away to a totally different kind of existence was sound then death would usually mean an enormous waste. A young man is educated for some particular work, engineering, architecture or statecraft, and graduates only perhaps to die soon afterward. All the time and energy spent in getting such an education would be largely lost either if death ends all, or is the last he will know of material things. Nature does not thus blunder. Her law of conservation is always operative. All the skill and wisdom acquired will be brought back in rebirth and will be used in the future incarnations.

A criticism that we sometimes hear is that since reincarnation gives us endless opportunity, there is no particular reason for living a noble life because there is always a chance to "make good" some time in the future. It is true that we shall have such opportunity as long as we need it and that is one of the most inspiring truths of nature; but since it is also true that all wrongdoing brings a harvest of pain and regret—since the real judgment day is sure and constant—there is no possible incentive to an evil course. No advantage that may be claimed for the restraining influence of the threat of a future hell is lacking in the hypothesis of reincarnation. The difference is that hell is vague and remote while reaction is definite and sure and therefore constitutes a more rational and effective restraint.

A child in school is a fair analogy for a soul in evolution. The child cannot get an education in a term nor in a year. He must return often to the same school, after the rest of regular vacations. He may use new books with higher lessons but he returns periodically to the same environment. In evolution the soul returns periodically to the physical plane for the same reasons. Continuous life here until all material experience is gained would be impossible. Aside from the need of the double process of acquiring and digesting experience, the physical body would become a hindrance to evolution. Within certain limits the physical brain can respond to the requirements of the growing soul but a new body is in time an absolute necessity to further evolution.

If we give a little thought to the evolutionary progress the ordinary person must make to raise him to mental and moral perfection, the inadequacy of a single lifetime becomes apparent. Consider, a moment, intellectual perfection. It would mean a development of the mind to the point of genius in many directions. If we combine into one mind the attainments of the mathematical genius, the musical genius, the inventive genius, the statecraft genius, and so on until every line of intellectual activity is included, we then have only the perfect mental man. On the moral side we must add to that the combined qualities of the saints. Then we have the perfected human being, with nothing more to be learned from incarnation here. His further evolution belongs to superphysical realms.

In trying to comprehend the evolution of the soul, that slowly changes it life after life from the savage to the civilized state and finally raises it to perfection, it is helpful to observe how that great work corresponds to the smaller cycle of a single lifetime. A great character in history begins life with helpless infancy. Steadily he progresses, unfolding new power at each step. He passes through the graded schools, slowly acquiring elementary lessons. College follows with higher and more difficult mental achievements. Then he enters business or professional life and begins to use his intellect with more and more initiative. He moves on into public life with its wider duties and responsibilities. From one post of honor he rises to another, with increasing ability and mastery, until at last he is the head of a nation and has become a world figure. Even so it is in the evolution of the soul. Life by life we rise, evolving new powers and virtues amidst ever-increasing opportunities and responsibilities. In one incarnation we have conditions that evolve courage. In another we are thrown into situations that develop tolerance. In still another we acquire patience and balance. In all of these incarnations we steadily evolve intellect and strengthen all previously acquired virtues. In each life we find the new conditions that are necessary for the exercise of our added abilities and, ultimately, with the powers, the spiritual insight and the ripened wisdom of the supermen themselves, we move forward to still higher fields, in superphysical evolution.

## CHAPTER X.

## REBIRTH: ITS JUSTICE

No matter how much we may differ in our views of the relationship between God and man there is general agreement about the attributes of the Supreme Being. All ascribe to Him unlimited power, wisdom, love and, of course, the perfection of all those desirable qualities that we see in human beings. The theosophical view is that all we see in man of power, wisdom, love, justice, beauty, harmony, are faint but actual manifestations of the attributes of the deity. All who are not materialists, denying the existence of a Supreme Being, will agree that the wisdom and justice of God must be perfect. It would be illogical and inconsistent to limit or qualify His attributes. Either He is all-wise and absolutely just, or else the materialist is right. We cannot have a deity at all unless He represents perfect justice.

Another point on which all but the materialists must agree is that creation is so ordered that the common welfare of humanity is best served by precisely the conditions of life that surround us. Nothing is different from what it should be unless it is because of man's failure to do what he should do for his own welfare. If it were otherwise what would become of the argument that an omniscient God has ordered it as it is? If, then, things are as they should be in the truest interests of man, and we find things in life that, according to our views of creation, are not right and just, it necessarily follows that the views we hold are erroneous.

The popular belief is that human beings constitute a special creation; that whenever a baby is born God creates a soul or individual consciousness for that body and that after a life of many years or a few, as the case may be, the body dies and the consciousness goes to dwell in remote regions forever. If the person lived a good life and also accepted the current religion he will be "saved" and will be eternally happy. If he lived an evil life but finally "believed" before death he will be saved anyway and be just as happy as though he had lived right from the start. If he did live a good life but rejected the current faith he will be lost and will be eternally miserable. According to this theory of special creation God makes people of all sorts. None of them can help being what they are created. Some are wise and some are foolish. Those who are wise enough to find the way of salvation will finally have heaven added to their original gift of wisdom. Those who are not created clever enough to find it will finally have hell added to their original endowment of stupidity! This is what some people are pleased to call divine justice!

It will hardly do to argue that the possibility that all may at last be happy in an endless heaven makes it unimportant that there are inequalities now. A vast majority of the theologians do not admit that such a state awaits the whole of the human race, and the comparatively few who do believe it will hardly venture to assert that present justice can be determined by future happiness. Even if we positively knew that eternal bliss awaited everybody after the close of this physical life how could that make it just that one person shall be born a congenital criminal and another shall be born a poet and philosopher? How could it make it right that one is born to life-long illness, suffering and poverty, while another has both wealth and a sound physical body? Not even the certainty of future happiness would be compensation for such present inequities. Why should there be any such inequalities if God represents unlimited power and perfect justice? Why should there be any poverty when, if He really created the soul itself instantaneously, He can as certainly create at once any necessary condition for the soul? Why poverty and disease and suffering at all? There must be a better answer to such questions than that "it pleased God to have it so." It is surely little better than blasphemy to suggest that any kind of unnecessary hard conditions for man are pleasing to the deity.

To hold that any future condition of happiness can make present justice out of the truly terrible inequalities of life, would be much like a millionaire who has two sons giving one of them all the advantages of wealth, travel, skilled instructors and special care, while the other was permitted to wear rags and go hungry. If the neglected son asked why he was thus treated while his brother was most carefully provided for, the father might reply with some indignation, "You are to have plenty in the future! My will is so drawn that when I die my great wealth will be equally divided between you and your brother. You will then be a millionaire with more money than you can possibly spend. So don't be foolish about your hardships now. Learn to starve like a gentleman!" The father's position in such a case would be just as reasonable as that of those who think a heaven hereafter can justify an earthly hell now.

Let us take some of the particular facts of life that puzzle us and test them with the hypothesis of special creation, and also with the hypothesis of reincarnation, and see which can explain them in a really satisfactory manner. In a Massachusetts prison, many years ago, died an old man whose name became familiar to many of us in our youth. He was then known as Jesse Pomeroy, the boy murderer. The present generation scarcely knows him. But in the latter part of the previous century he was the sensation of the times. For the crime of murdering his playmates the boy was sent to prison for life. Why did Pomeroy become a noted criminal in childhood? If the theory of special creation is sound he was created and put in the world to fit himself for a future heaven. But he was created in such fashion that he was deficient in moral perception and he began life with an act that led to his expulsion from society. If God created this soul as we first knew him why was he not created with the moral balance of a law-abiding citizen so that he could have lived long and peacefully in civilized society and have been prepared for heaven at death? What could have been the purpose of giving him a brain that could not think soundly and a conscience that welcomed murder? That leads invariably to the question, Why are criminals created at all? Why are idiots created? The deeper we look into the facts of life the more unsatisfactory does the theory of special creation become because we find a thousand things that contradict it and show its inconsistency. If the purpose of God was to create a heaven to be enjoyed by those who reach it we cannot see why He should create a humanity the majority of which is incapable of ever attaining it. If He creates them as they come into the world at birth why are not all of them created wise and kind? Why must most of them blunder through life, making all sorts of mistakes, bringing suffering to others by their unkindness or cruelty only, in the end, to pass from a life of failure to eternal punishment for that failure? There is no reason, no justice in such a theory.

Let us turn to the explanation of reincarnation. According to that, Pomeroy has had many past incarnations and will have many more. Like all the rest of us he came up from primitive man. We have all learned the lessons of civilized life slowly by experience like children acquiring lessons from their books. The majority have come along well and have developed a fair share of intellect in dealing with life's problems, and some degree of sympathy for others. Some have evolved rapidly like hard working pupils and they are called geniuses. Some have lagged behind and have learned very little. They are like the truants at school who have broken the rules and run away from their lessons. These laggards of the human race are the dullards and the criminals, who have moved so slowly incarnation after incarnation, or are so much younger in evolution, that they are now bringing savage traits into our present civilized life.

Reincarnation not only explains who and what the criminal is but it also explains away the hell with which the theory of special creation threatens him. No hell awaits him except that which he has created himself by what he has done. By the law of cause and effect all the cruelty and suffering he has inflicted will react upon him to his sorrow, but will also serve for his enlightenment. In his next incarnation the kind of body he will have and the environment in which he will live will be determined exactly by the thoughts and emotions and acts of this and past incarnations. He will therefore neither go to a heaven for which he is not yet fitted nor to an eternal hell which he does not deserve. He will simply come back in another physical body and have a chance to try it again, but he will have to make the trial under the conditions which his conduct merits.

And what of the idiot? According to the hypothesis of special creation we cannot possibly explain him. It would be blasphemous to believe that God creates a mindless man. If one soul is given a mind and another is not, and for no reason whatever, it is the most monstrous injustice that ever challenged the understanding of man! Think for a moment of the difference between the idiot and the normal person. The man of sound mind has before him the opportunity of progress, of mental and moral development. The avenues of business and professional life are open before him. He is free to try his powers and win his way. Wealth, power and fame are all possible for him. All the joys of social life may be his. Think of him surrounded by his family and friends, successful, satisfied, happy, and then think of the life of the idiot. Language cannot express the horror of the contrast! If there were no other explanation of life than that of special creation it would change the world into the hopeless hell of a madhouse. Again reincarnation saves us from either blasphemy or madness. The idiot, like the cripple, differs from the normal man only in the body, which is the instrument of the soul. Deformity of the body is a limitation of the ego who functions through it. A withered arm, a clubfoot, a deformed back, in this incarnation are results of unfortunate causes which that soul has generated in past lives. In idiocy the malformation is in the brain. Of course this is not an accident. There is no element of chance which places the limitation in one body where it causes but minor trouble and in another where it prevents mental activity and thus produces idiocy. In each case it is the exact working out of the law. The body of the idiot is the physical plane expression of a soul that has made a serious blunder in the past, possibly by limiting another with cruel restraint, and the gross misuse of his intellect and power in that way has operated to prevent his using it at all in the present life. Such limitations belong to the outer planes. It is the form that limits and when the form perishes the limitation disappears. As with the criminal, no hell is needed to punish the idiot. He has made his own hell by his mistake in the past and in this incarnation he must live in it and expiate his blunder. Perhaps it may seem to some that since the idiot is incapable of realizing the life of the normal person the situation represents no real misfortune for him; but idiocy on the physical plane does not mean idiocy in the soul. Even from the astral plane the ego may keenly feel the horror of functioning for a lifetime through such a physical body, as one here would feel the anguish of incarceration in a dungeon.

The criminal and the idiot are striking illustrations of the failure of the theory of special creation to explain the facts of life satisfactorily; but if we turn to the other extreme and consider the most fortunate people in the world we shall find there, too, precisely the same failure to explain. By the hypothesis of special creation we find a gross injustice done to the soul born an ignoramus. Yet we find others possessing intelligence in superabundance.

In the same city where the genius is born we find the idiot. Did God create them both as they were born or did they come up to their present difference of mental equipment through a process of evolution that accounts for it all satisfactorily? If the theory of special creation is sound why did not the idiot get at least a little of the intellect that the genius could so easily have spared? If they are the work of special creation it is impossible to find reason or justice in such terrible inequalities; but if reincarnation is God's method of creation the explanation of the difference between them becomes simple. The genius is not only an old soul but evidently one who has worked hard in past lives, overcoming lassitude and evolving the power of will that enabled him to triumph over obstacles, conquering all the enemies of intellectual progress and thus evolving the fine brain he now possesses. His present abilities are but the sum total of the energies he has put forth in the past.

The theory of special creation does not explain the facts of life. It is not in accord with natural law. Nature knows no such thing as special creation. To believe in special creation is to ignore all scientific facts and principles. Reincarnation is evolution and every kingdom of nature develops through evolution. The difference between the shriveled wild grain that, ages ago, struggled with the rock and soil for sustenance enough to reproduce itself, and the plump wheat of the cultivated fields that today feeds the world, is the work of evolution. The wild stalk produced the seed and from that seed came a better stalk. The better stalk produced a still better kernel and from that sprang a superior stalk to yield a higher grade of wheat than any of its predecessors. The stalk sprouts from the ground, matures, stores all its gain of growth within the seed and perishes; but from the seed springs its reincarnated form, to repeat the process that changes poor to good, good to better and better into best. And thus it is with the reincarnating soul. As the almost worthless grain through countless seasons is slowly changed to perfect worth, the soul is by that same law of evolution slowly changed through many incarnations from the chaos of savage instincts to the law and order of the moral world. Each incarnation yields some improvement. As the grain sprouts within the darkness of the soil and, perishing there, attains its full results in the higher realm of air and sun, drawing from the soil that which, stored within the surviving seed, gives power to reproduce its better self, so the soul takes anchorage in the lower planes and draws from its varied experiences here that which, transmuted after the body's death, gives the power to return with greater life.

Attempts have been made to find some explanation of the mental and moral inequalities that exist at birth. In the earlier days of the study of evolution it was usually asserted that the human being inherits his mentality and morality from his parents; but even if that were true the injustice of one being born a genius and another a fool would remain. It is the inequality that constitutes the injustice, and it is of no importance whether it comes about through heredity or otherwise; but as a matter of fact heredity is confined to the physical side of existence. As more and more is learned by observation the old theory of mental and moral heredity has lost ground until it can now be said that it has no recognition in the scientific world.

In the absence of evidence that either mental or moral traits are transmitted to offspring, one naturally turns to the observations of those having some practical experience. Dr. A. Ritter, of the Stanford University Children's Clinic, who had large numbers of defective children in charge, treating no less than sixteen hundred in a single year says:

"As to the definite causes of the prevalence of defective types, I cannot speak with finality or assurance. I do not agree with social or educational doctrinaires who assign the causes definitely to liquor, poverty, infectious diseases, or other social or moral shortcomings. The greatest minds of the world are hesitant in theorizing about this. There is a complexity of causes which explains many of these cases, but no generalization fits absolutely. We may find a case which is not traceable to any of these conditions—a case in which the antecedents would promise a perfectly normal child, and yet we are confronted with a defective child. On the other hand, bright, normal children, even children of superior intelligence sometimes spring from such conditions."*

A little reasoning about the facts concerning both genius and idiocy will make it clear that neither is inherited. If it were true that genius is inherited, society would present a different appearance. There would be famous families of geniuses living in the world—geniuses in music, in poetry, in warfare, in invention, in art. The fact is that it is difficult to find even two geniuses in any family. Caesar, Napoleon, Edison, Wagner, Shakespeare, stand alone with neither great forbears nor great descendants.

---

* Interview in *San Francisco Examiner*

We search in vain for famous ancestors of such men; but if the theory of mental heredity is sound we should know their ancestors for precisely the same reason that we know them.

Heredity, then, does not explain whence genius comes; and if anybody had really traced genius from father, or grandfather, to son or grandson, we should still have no explanation of what genius is. The only reason why it appears so incomprehensible is because we have not looked at it in the light of nature's truth. We have erroneously assumed that this is the only life we live on the physical plane, and therefore the time is too short for the evolution of genius. A man can become an expert in one lifetime but not a genius. If we give him many incarnations to develop along certain lines he can become a genius. The soul that works strenuously at building up a certain faculty through many incarnations naturally develops qualities that shine out brilliantly upon its return to a physical body and we have the genius. We evolve our mentality and morality, and there could be no justice in life if it were otherwise.

It is important to distinguish between mental and moral heredity, and physical heredity. The latter is, of course, well established. Insanity and certain diseases run in families and are sometimes handed on from parents to children; but these things are not of the Self; they relate, not to the soul, but to the soul's vehicle. There is no insanity in any soul but only some malformation in one or more parts of the mechanism through which it functions.

It is commonly said that a person inherits some

disease or at least a tendency that will develop it as, for example, tuberculosis. But what has really occurred is that, in his reincarnation he has been drawn, by the operation of natural laws, into a family that can give him a physical body with such power of resistance, or the lack of it, as he is entitled to. If certain parents could give a reincarnating soul only a weak body or a defective brain, or both, then a soul whose past does not merit such a fate simply could not be drawn into that family; but the hypothesis that any two parents must necessarily endow their offspring with such bodies should be used with caution. We commonly see great diversity in families; weak parents with strong progeny, brothers and sisters representing all degrees of constant health and chronic illness, fathers and mothers with children endowed with mental capacity far beyond their parents, and also normal and brilliant parents with children that are stupid or idiotic. Obviously the laws that determine such things go much deeper than physical relationship and are too complex to be explained solely by physical heredity.

Sometimes people who do not clearly understand reincarnation say they do not like the idea because next time they might not get the kind of body they would like. Some even fear that they might get the body of a savage! Since the body is always the material expression of the soul, of one's own deathless self, one's next incarnation must necessarily be all that he now is in thought and emotion, intellect and morality, plus all he shall evolve between now and his next appearance here. If we have understanding of the relation between the physical body and the spiritual body, we must see that exact law and not chance governs the whole matter. To understand rightly the theosophical idea of old souls in new bodies one must have clearly in mind the imperishable individuality of the soul. It is originally a spark of the divine life and through the evolution of a vast period of time that spark becomes a flame. From the time it is the spark it undergoes experiences that are unlike the experiences of any other soul, and these give it an individuality that is never lost. When it has risen high enough to enter the human kingdom and has expanded to what we call the human soul, it then goes forward in its evolution to super-human levels by getting the experiences in a succession of physical bodies that develop its latent divinity, and each body is something of an improvement on the last. In a given incarnation the man thinks and feels and acts, and the forces he thus generates must have their reactions. Some of the reactions take place immediately but others are long deferred; and thus a chain of cause and effect connects all the lives in the whole evolutionary journey of the soul. Each incarnation is as definitely the result of preceding incarnations as our todays are definitely related to our yesterdays. What we think and feel and do in this life, plus what we were at the beginning of this life, exactly determines what we shall be in the next one. To get a body in our next incarnation that is not precisely representative of one's self is as impossible as it is that a man who has been a surgeon or an artist all his life should awaken tomorrow with only the ability to be a fruit vendor on the street; or that a bootblack, who has never known any other occupation, should find himself tomorrow able to take up the work of the chemist or the statesman.

If a soul that has evolved the ability to think deeply, like a great scientist or a philosopher, could come back in a body that had the brain of a very commonplace man, it would be impossible for such a brain to express that soul's wisdom and so all the hard study of the past would be lost for that incarnation. His knowledge would be useless here. Sometimes just that does occur through the evil course followed by a soul in a previous incarnation, as in idiocy. In such a case the real man, the soul, would not be less wise than in the past. He would merely be afflicted with a body for the time being through which he could not possibly express that wisdom. At each birth in a new body the old soul brings into action, as rapidly as the new infant brain develops, the skill and wisdom acquired in previous lives, provided there is no restricting factor arising out of past wrongdoing that constitutes a temporary limitation.

There is no element of chance in getting a new physical body in the next incarnation. The body is the material expression of the self. It is as much the product of the self as the rose is of the bush, the apple of the tree, or the tulip of the bulb. The musician can no more get a body suitable to the blacksmith than the rose bush can produce wheat or oats. We do not get bodies by lottery, like destitute people drawing clothing by numbers which might result in grotesque misfits. We do not receive bodies at all. We *evolve* them, and in each incarnation the new body represents all the soul has come to be up to that point in its evolution. Such a view of life has a basis of absolute justice. Every soul has exactly what it has earned.

The old theory of but one physical lifetime is devoid of consistency as well as of justice. The common belief in Occidental civilization is that we live here for only sixty or seventy years and that, when we die, we pass on to live eternally somewhere else, and that the whole of eternity, whether it is filled with pleasure or is horrible with pain, is made to depend upon how we spent those few years of the physical life! Such a fate would be unfair and unjust. If a schoolboy is incorrigible for a term it would not be fair to condemn him to lose all opportunity of education. We would give him another chance at the following term.

A little incident of disobedience from home life will illustrate the point. A quinine capsule was lying on the table. A three-year-old boy reached for it. His mother called across the room, "Don't eat that, it isn't good;" but in a spirit of reckless mischief he hurried it into his mouth and quickly crushed it. It was a very disagreeable but salutary lesson for the little fellow. It is an example of nature's methods. She is always consistent, with a balanced relationship between cause and effect. But suppose in this case we throw her consistency aside as those who believe that eternal results will follow temporal effects are obliged to do. An ordinary life-

## REBIRTH: ITS JUSTICE

time compared to eternity is somewhat like that instant of disobedience compared to a long physical life; but the illustration is not adequate because eternity never ends. As nearly as the principle can be applied it would be by saying to the child, "Because you were disobedient for a second of time you shall taste quinine until you die!" If that punishment is injustice what must we call the infliction of an eternity of pain as the results of the errors committed in a lifetime?

Any hypothesis of existence that does not take into consideration the welfare of humanity is a false hypothesis. What plan can better serve the common welfare than a chance to redeem a failure? When a prisoner is condemned for a crime we do not deprive him of opportunities. We give him every possible chance to improve his character. Rebirth is another chance. Every incarnation is a new opportunity.

If the popular idea of an eternal heaven and hell is sound, the time will come when the majority of the race will have used their one opportunity of a brief lifetime, and have failed. If that were really true, it is easy to imagine what they would do with another opportunity if they had it! How long should opportunity be given? Just as long as it will be used, and to deprive anybody of it when he is eager to redeem past errors is to ignore the essentials of human welfare. Therefore such a plan cannot be the true one. John J. Ingalls personified opportunity and wrote:

Master of human destinies am I!
    Fame, Love and Fortune on my footsteps wait;
    Cities and fields I walk; I penetrate
Deserts and seas remote, and passing by
    Hovel and mart and palace, soon or late
    I knock unbidden once at every gate.
If sleeping, wake; if feasting, rise before
    I turn away. It is the hour of fate,
    And they who follow me reach every state
Mortals desire, and conquer every foe
    Save Death; but those who doubt or hesitate,
Condemned to failure, penury and woe,
    Seek me in vain and uselessly implore;
    I answer not and I return no more.

That is true enough from one viewpoint and profitably emphasizes the importance of acting promptly when the time for action arrives; but there is another truth to be expressed on the subject and it is well done by Walter Malone, who says:

They do me wrong who say I come no more,
    When once I knock and fail to find you in;
For every day I stand outside your door,
    And bid you wake and rise to fight and win.
Wail not for precious chances passed away;
    Weep not for golden ages on the wane;
Each night I burn the records of the day;
    At sunrise every soul is born again.
Laugh like a boy at splendors that are sped;
    To vanished joys be blind and deaf and dumb;
My judgments seal the dead past with its dead,
    But never bind a moment yet to come.
Though deep in mire, wring not your hands and weep,
I lend my arm to all who say, "I can."

What a magnificent view of human evolution!

No ultimate failure possible because there is always another chance. The failures of one incarnation made good by the sincere efforts of the next! All the faults and frailties—the shadow blots of the past —vanishing in the light of a higher wisdom that has been won. No endless hell, no eternal torment; not even the ghosts of vanished chances to haunt the mind; but only the insistent voice of immortal Opportunity, urging us to wake and rise to strive and win!

## CHAPTER XI.

## REBIRTH: ITS NECESSITY

There are apparently but three ways in which anybody has attempted to explain the origin of the race. One of the three theories is that of the materialist. Another is the common belief that God created an original human pair and continues to create souls equal to the number of babies born into the world. The third hypothesis is that of the evolution of the soul.

The materialist's position seems to be, briefly, that the forces of nature, with no directive intelligence, are sufficient to account for man as we see him; that consciousness after death is a delusion; that immortality is a vain dream and that the human being has neither a past nor a future life.

This materialistic belief regards the human body as a self-sufficient machine with a brain that generates thought; but the savage has a completely developed physical body with eyes, ears and other organs like our own. His brain has the same structure as the brain of civilized man. Indeed, his physical body is not only as complete a machine as ours but is likely to be materially sounder. Why, then, if the brain produces thought, does not this savage produce the thoughts of a philosopher? If there is no directing soul back of the brain, why the marvelous difference in the product of the two brains?

Materialists do not explain the phenomena of life. They can talk learnedly about it but they must stop short of the source of life. Everything about anatomy and physiology they know, but the life that flows through the human machine remains unexplained. They can trace the circulation of the blood from the heart through the arteries, from the arteries to the veins, from the veins back to the heart, but the greatest mind the race has produced cannot say what makes the heart beat. Life has not been explained and cannot be explained from the materialist's viewpoint. With marvelous instruments and wondrous skill science has explored and mapped and charted the "tabernacle of clay," but it cannot throw a single ray of light upon the source of the intelligence that animates it.

Materialism fails sadly enough in that direction, but still worse as a satisfactory interpretation of the panorama of life about us. It is a philosophy of the gloomiest fatalism. It holds that we simply chance to be that which we are; that we are what we are merely because of fortuitous chemical and mechanical combinations. Had the combinations chanced to be something different we should not be in existence. According to this theory all abilities are the gifts of nature and all lack of them is the blind work of chance. No credit whatever is due to anybody for what he was at birth nor can anybody logically be blamed for his deficiencies.

This hypothesis holds that recently we were not

and that presently we shall cease to be; that we appear by chance, live our brief period, suffer or enjoy as it may happen and then pass to the oblivion of the dust; that all the thought, all the toil and the striving, all the effort and endurance were for nothing, and accomplished nothing. Such a philosophy will not long survive the progress of our age. It lacks the element of justice that is enthroned in every human consciousness and without which life would be a meaningless mockery and the world a chaos of despair.

However, the materialist's philosophy has no monopoly of bad points or undesirable beliefs. The old popular idea of a mechanical creation is equally at war with both fact and reason. That belief is that God created the earth as men build houses, and added the human beings as men furnish their houses when built. It is the belief that souls begin their existence at birth, live here but one life and then pass on into either endless bliss or eternal pain.

This idea differs from materialism in the matter of a governing intelligence and on the point of immortality but it is remarkably like it in other ways. It merely puts an intelligent force as first cause where the materialist postulates blind force.

The materialist says that all human characteristics are the gift of nature while according to the popular belief they are the gifts of God. In either case some human beings get abilities they have not earned and others are afflicted with defects they do not deserve. The intellectual man is favored without reason and the fool is handicapped without mercy.

Some come into the world with salvation assured by being well born while others are foredoomed to failure. Predestination goes logically with such ideas. Happily the world has long been growing away from the once wide-spread belief in predestination because it is too shocking to the modern sense of justice; yet if there is but one life on earth and the soul is created at birth, the very essence of predestination remains, because some are created with the wisdom to attain salvation and others are created without it.

If the soul has no pre-existence it can have no responsibility at the time of birth. Neither can it have any merit. One is born with a sound mind and moral insight. These qualities lead to salvation but the man has done nothing to earn them. Another is born with cruel and vicious tendencies and a poor intellect. He may therefore miss salvation, but if he had no pre-existence he can have done nothing to deserve such a start in life. If we are really here for the first time then justice can be done only by giving us equal equipment at the start and equal opportunities afterward.

The difference between human beings at birth is enormous. There is every degree of vice and virtue from the savage to the saint and every mental variation from the fool to the philosopher. If God really creates the soul at birth, then one is created wise and kind though he did nothing to earn it. Another is created vicious and depraved. He did nothing to deserve it. One is showered with "natural gifts" to which he is not justly entitled. Another is blighted with a stupidity he did nothing to incur;

and we are asked to believe that thus they were created!

It is easy to see why, in that old view of the relationship between God and man, salvation was to be by faith. It was impossible for a person to be saved by his merit because, if he was created with his qualities, he had no merit. His very ability to comprehend spiritual truth and his moral strength to resist temptation were conferred upon him, not evolved by him. If that popular view is sound, human beings should be neither praised nor censured. They are simply human automata operated by such degree of mental and moral ability as God chose to assign to them. If that be true, genius should have no credit for its accomplishments, indolence no frown of disapproval, cowardice no lash of condemnation, tolerance no meed of praise, cruelty no rebuke, virtue no applause, and heroism no fame for its selfless sacrifice. And yet that absurd and illogical belief lingers in the minds of millions of people. It is believed merely because it always has been believed! It is a mass inheritance from the Middle Ages.

If materialism is an impossible philosophy, then the popular belief that the soul is created at birth is impossible. It is a theory that encumbers its belief in immortality with conditions that destroy justice and defy logic. That old form of belief has outlived its day. It was possible at any time only because there was too little information and, like the old belief that the world was flat, it must yield place to the newer knowledge. The truth of evolution is the staunchest friend of religion. It is the foundation on which may be built a scientific belief in a Supreme Being, a rational faith in immortality and a brotherhood of man that has a basis in nature itself.

What are some of the truths that evolution has taught us and how do they give evidence against materialism and in support of the theosophical hypothesis?

Evolution is an orderly unfolding from the single to the diversified, from the simple to the complex, in which process life evolves by passing from lower to higher forms and storing within itself the gist of the experiences gained in each.

One of the vital facts that evolution establishes is that slow building is the order of creation. The horse is an example. He is traced backward with certainty to a small creature that resembles him very little indeed. Ages were required to evolve the horse to his present intelligence and utility. Another profoundly important fact in evolution is the continuity of life from body to body. The butterfly is frequently used as an illustration, but the principle holds with other insects. In the metamorphosis of the caterpillar we have a phenomenon so common that many people have personally observed it. Watch, in imagination, its transformation. The worm is a physical body occupied by evolving life. Its physical body perishes and becomes part of the dust of the street. The life enters the tomb of the chrysalis. The experimenting scientist takes that chrysalis, packs it in an icehouse and leaves it frozen for more than a year. A mere frost will kill either caterpillar or butterfly, but when the chrysalis is removed from the ice and brought into a higher temperature in due time the triumphant life emerges in the form of the butterfly. This phenomenon shows that life does survive the loss of the body. The body of the caterpillar is dead and has turned to dust, but the caterpillar that lived in it is not dead. It now lives again in the material world in a physical body of a higher type.

Here, in an order of existence almost infinitely below man, we have life existing in a physical form, passing from it and, after a very long period, expressing itself through a higher form. Who can admit such continuity of life for the insect and deny it for man? Can there be a deathless something in a worm and not in a human being? Even without the mass of physical evidence that exists upon the subject the logic of nature would lead us to confident conclusions. The knowledge of evolution which science has so far accumulated leads to some natural inferences. One is that man is immortal. Another is that he has, like all creatures, slowly evolved to what he now is. A third is that both life, and the forms it uses, are evolving together; and another is that lower orders evolve into higher and continually higher ones. The human soul evolves from the savage to the saint—from animal instincts to the self-sacrifice of martyrs and heroes. We cannot escape the conclusion that the race has evolved, is evolving and will continue to evolve until mental and moral perfection has been attained.

If neither the theory of the materialist nor the

popular notion that the soul is created at birth is satisfactory, we have only reincarnation left as a working hypothesis; and if we regard the evolution of the soul as a natural truth, then reincarnation becomes a necessity in explaining the known facts of life.

Those who desire to put their ideas about the soul and its immortality into harmony with the truths of evolution sometimes ask why it would not be possible for the soul to leave the material plane forever at the death of the physical body and then pursue its evolution on higher planes. In the vast universe there must be opportunity for all possible development, it is argued.

Why go on into other regions when the lessons here have not been learned? The average human being is in the elementary grades, with many incarnations ahead of him before he will be in a position even to take advantage of all his opportunities here and thus make fairly rapid progress. To talk of going on to higher planes for further evolution is like proposing that a child shall leave the kindergarten and enter the university.

We are evolving mentally and morally and a little consideration of the matter will make clear two important points—that we have much to learn and that the physical plane is wonderfully arranged for our instruction. We have conditions here for developing mentality that do not exist on higher planes. The absolute necessity of procuring food is an example. Death is the penalty for failure to obtain it. Hunger was the earliest spur to action at the low level of evolution and even now at our comparatively high point of attainment it is one of the chief factors of racial activity. In providing the necessities of life and in gratifying our multitude of desires mentality is developed. Business and professional life rests upon these physical plane necessities and, engaged in solving the problems of civilization, the race evolves intellect. Such problems do not, of course, exist on higher planes.

While the mentality is thus being pushed along in evolution by our material necessities the heart qualities are developed by the family ties in a way that could not be done elsewhere. In the nature of things the entrance of the soul to the physical plane is attended with helplessness. From the beginning it must have material necessities or die, and yet it can do nothing in its new infant body. Again, as a rule, long before it leaves the physical plane old age has once more rendered it helpless. Thus every human soul must depend on the assistance of others at two critical periods of each incarnation. The help it receives, in infancy and old age, it pays back to the race, in the care of both the helpless young and the helpless old, when it is in the vigor of mature physical life. It is obvious that such experience develops the qualities of sympathy and compassion as no phase of business life could. The relationship of parent and child, husband and wife, evolves the heart qualities in a way that would be impossible in the totally different environment of higher planes. Naturally enough, each plane has a specific work to do in the soul's evolution. We can no more learn in the highest planes the lessons the material world is designed to teach us than a pupil can acquire a knowledge of mathematics from his lessons in geography. Hence the necessity for a periodical return to physical life until its experiences have developed in us the qualities we lack.

Not only has each plane its special adaptability to particular needs of the soul in its evolution, but the two kinds of physical bodies—masculine and feminine—through which the soul functions, afford special advantages for acquiring the lessons of life. The soul on its home plane is, of course, sexless. Sex, as we know it, is a differentiation arising from the soul's expression on lower planes. All characteristics of the soul itself, such as intelligence, love, or devotion, are common to both sexes.

The ego functioning through the masculine body has the opportunity of certain experiences that would be impossible in the feminine body, while, of course, the feminine form enables the soul to get experience that could not be obtained in a masculine body. A consideration of the widely different experiences of fathers and mothers, sons and daughters, will show how true this is. The lessons learned in the masculine body are largely those of the head while in the feminine form they are lessons of the heart.

When the ego puts forth its energies and begins descent into lower planes for another incarnation it is apparently beginning a cycle of experience in which either mentality or spirituality shall be the dominant note for that incarnation, and probably for several others. If it is to evolve for the time being through those experiences related to objective activity, with intellect as the guiding factor, the masculine body can best serve the purpose; if the dominant note is to be spirituality rather than mentality, and the soul is, for the time, moving along the line of the heart side—the subjective, the intuitive—then the feminine body is the better vehicle in which such experience can be obtained. To say that mentality is the dominant factor of masculine incarnation does not at all mean that men have a monopoly of the reasoning faculty; nor does the fact that other souls are being expressed through the feminine body mean that they have a fundamental spiritual advantage. Some women are better reasoners than some men, while some men are more spiritual than some women. What it does mean is that for the time being the ego is expressing itself dominantly along a certain line.

Our ordinary language confirms the truth of the statement that men normally express more of the head qualities and women more of the heart qualities. We speak of men as being reasoners and of women as being intuitional and depending upon their impressions. The soul in the masculine body is for the time being getting experiences of the outer, objective activities. He is the home builder and protector, the bread winner, the battle fighter. The soul in the feminine body is, for the time, getting experience along the line of the inner life. She is the wife, sister and mother, and her lessons are of the heart rather than the head.

As we study nature we are more and more impressed with the wonderful mechanism for the evolution of the soul. It soon becomes clear to the student that every individual is, in each incarnation, thrown into precisely the circumstances required for the greatest possible progress of that particular ego. If the qualities of initiative and courage are to be developed, the masculine body admirably serves the purpose, while if sympathy and compassion need stimulation the feminine form is wonderfully effective for that kind of progress. It requires little reasoning to see that the soul would not continue to incarnate in one sex indefinitely. It must develop all its inner qualities. Both intellect and compassion must reach perfect expression. Such a consummation can, of course, be best attained by alternating sex experiences; but here again there is wide latitude in the operation of the law. The rule seems to be that ordinarily there are not less than three nor more than seven successive incarnations in one sex, and then the ego begins to express itself through a body of the other sex. By that rule it would commonly be for a period of from a few hundred years to some thousands of years, that the ego expresses itself through one sex before it changes to the other; but here again we must remember that we are speaking of general rules applied to groups of souls and that there are many exceptions to such generalities.

While the necessity for rebirth has its many specific details it may be placed broadly on the statement that since even the longest lifetime is not sufficient for acquiring all the physical realm can teach us, many incarnations are required to complete the soul's material education. The more one ponders the subject the clearer does it become that reincarnation is the necessary method of the soul's progress from lowly levels to the heights of spiritual wisdom and power.

The idea of the immanence of God and the direct relationship of man to Him is a viewpoint from which all the facts of life can be rationally explained. By it we can show that this fragment of the whole that we call physical life exhibits wisdom and justice, and that the totality which we call the universe has the elements of success and happiness; but the popular misconception that God is external to His universe, gets one into all sorts of difficulties. It is the mechanical conception that makes the trouble. It is the idea that God is a manufacturer of souls, producing them as a factory turns out tables and chairs; but how then can we explain the tremendous difference between the various grades of the output and the presence on the earth of such a lot of useless furniture!* Take as an example such human beings as the primitive types of man. If God instantaneously created the earth and its contents and if He started it as many believe with a Garden of Eden and Adam and Eve as the progenitors of the race, why these beings of the present day? Tens of thousands of them are born every year. If God creates the soul

---

*The most primitive of peoples possess qualities potential of later development. Experiences in many cultures are useful and are necessary for humanity's evolutionary unfoldment.

when it appears here in a physical body, *why* does He create savages? And why, at our own level of life are thousands of fools and idiots created? The old view assumes that although there is an all-wise God Who creates and manages the universe He does it in such a haphazard way that it is a mere matter of chance whether one is born a genius or a fool. According to vital statistics in the last twelve months many millions of babies were born in the world. Did God create souls for those bodies? If He did, why did He make so many of them stupid instead of intelligent? Why did He make the majority of them commonplace instead of brilliant? Why did He endow some with intelligence so keen and morality so sound that they are certain to have successful and happy lives while others are given minds that are baffled by simple problems, and a moral will so feeble that it will certainly fail them in the temptations they meet?

A competent workman is known by his product. What would one think of an expert machinist who made some excellent machines, but who turned out a majority that were decidedly inferior to the best he could make, and occasionally put out a machine that instead of being useful destroyed everything in its vicinity? If God creates souls as a manufacturer makes furniture, why did He create Socrates for Athens and Nero for Rome? Why did He produce souls like Shakespeare and Emerson and Whitman and then for every such moral giant create a thousand fools and destroyers?

Of course, the Supreme Being does not make

blunders. It is because people create an imaginary God that there is any inconsistency. Their hypothesis is wrong and that is why the facts as we see them about us will not "square" with it. He does, indeed, create all these things, but not in the very least as men make material objects. His method of creation is evolutionary. He involves His life in the solar system and it then evolves and slowly brings its latent mental and moral powers into expression. The natural savage like the cannibal, and the civilized savage like some of the inhuman destroyers in history, are both expressions of His life; but they are partial expressions. The natural savage is a very young soul. He is only a step above the animal kingdom. Intellect and morality are just dawning in him. He is no more to be censured because he does not live our kind of life than a cat should be blamed for its inability to understand the commandments. A tyrant is an old soul. Intellect is well developed in him, but he has evolved in unbalanced fashion. Moral unfoldment has not kept pace with mental development. It is only on the intellectual side that he is exhibiting the divine qualities that are latent in every human being; but in some degree his moral faculties must also be developed. We get an exaggerated idea of his moral side—or more accurately speaking his immoral side—because we are appalled by the horrors for which he is responsible. When we study closely the life of some of the exponents of military force we often find an apparent lack of heart qualities. Intellect may attain high development while the moral forces still lie latent, but somewhere in the future incarnations, out of all the great suffering that comes to one who loves war for its own sake, compassion will be born and keen sympathy for all humanity will spring into being. The divine spark is in all, from the savage to the cultured, from the despot to the saint.

If civilized people are old souls in new bodies, it is easy to account for things as we see them. If the soul is old we can understand the wisdom it sometimes exhibits even in childhood. We can comprehend prodigies. We can explain genius. If the divine life is latent in all, but can be evolved only through a long series of incarnations, we can also account for all degrees of selfishness and cruelty in civilized people by the irregularity of the development. In short, we can understand an imperfect world as the creation of a perfect Being, because that world is still in process of creation. It is like a house during the period of its construction. There is a stage when it is only half a house. The floors are not laid, the doors are not hung, the windows are not set; but we do not complain, because we know that the house is still in the process of building. We do not rail at the carpenters because it is incomplete. We know that there is a necessary time relationship between the plan of the architect and the working out of his ideas in wood and iron and stone and mortar. In precisely the same sense, humanity is incomplete. It is still in the process of its evolutionary creation. Thus we can account for the imperfections in that which is essentially divine; for the mingled wisdom and ignorance, for the injustice and cruelty, for the happiness and the sorrow, for the success and the failures.

If it were not so, if humanity sprang into being through instantaneous creation, it would be impossible to explain why the world is full of apparent blunders. Even a man, given infinite power with only a man's intelligence, could make a better world. He could make seas without treacherous reefs, continents without deserts, forests without deadly serpents. A witty critic of old fashioned beliefs was once challenged to say how he could have made a better world if he had the power. He replied, "Well, for one thing, I would have made good health catching instead of disease!" Other improvements we can think of, if humanity had really been instantaneously created; but it was not. The evolutionary process of creation is still going on and that is just why there will be the unpleasant side of physical life as long as any portion of the divinity within remains latent. To put it differently, the earth is a mental and moral training ground, especially designed to evolve us. If there were no dangers to face, courage could not be evolved. If there were no suffering, there would be no sympathy. If there were no temptations, we should never attain self-mastery. There must be a mechanism through which the latent divinity in man can become active as certainly as there must be mechanism by which the athlete develops his strength. Without a point of resistance his muscles could not be improved. He would remain a man but he would never be an athlete. Without the rigors of physical life with all its heartaches and difficulties, we would remain human but we would not become supermen and masters of nature.

The human soul is an actor in the great drama of physical life. He has played many roles from the trivial to the great. He has known a score of civilizations in every clime, and type of land, from seagirt plains to rugged mountain heights. He has lived the primitive life where patriotism had its birth in the battles of the tribes. He has been a chief of savage men and led his warriors in the fray. He has lived amid lurking dangers that thrilled his latent senses into life, and in the desert wilds has matched his skill and courage against the king of beasts. He has known the lonely forest depths and in the hush of night has gazed in wonder toward the solemn silence of the stars; and by it all, thought was aroused and strength and skill and courage were evolved. Thus many times he lived and died.

Then came a wider reach of life with reason slowly rising above the instincts of the brute. He was born in the lowest levels of civil life, where wild emotions must answer to the law. Reaction followed swiftly upon its cause. He struck the murderer's vengeful blow, and became the fleeing criminal. He felt the iron hand of justice close upon his arm. He heard the judge pronounce his doom and lived through the hell of passing days until he met a felon's death.

With slowly growing comprehension he was reborn, scores of times, to civil life. In each he learned some things. He was lured onward by desire, he was driven by the lash of need. He ran the gamut of emotions from ecstacy to woe. He has been the free citizen surrounded with genial friends, he has also been the plotter of insurrections, and has finished life with a galley slave's despair. He may have looked upon the beauty of ancient Greece. He has been a citizen of mighty Rome. He has heard her orators in the forum, has mingled in the arena's cruel throng and has seen the lion's victim torn to shreds. He has been a soldier in the field, marching with the legions of the Caesars, where untamed emotions were brought within the iron discipline of war.

He has slowly risen to posts of honor and authority. If well advanced in evolution, he may have been both worker and manager, the subject and the ruler. He has felt the pinch of poverty and has known the cares of state. He has been both pupil and teacher and has caught a gleam of immortal hope, only to lose it in reason's tortuous course. He has ascended the heights of aspiration and has plodded through the valleys of despair; and at last he awakened to life's real purpose and set himself to the task of self-mastery, the mightiest battle of all his lives!

Then onward and upward, incarnation after incarnation, he rises in evolution's scale with expanding intellect and increasing power, amid the higher and finer experiences where the last and best of moral strength and courage are evolved; and, when at last the final curtain falls, he has become the superman—master of himself and of nature's wondrous forces.

## CHAPTER XII.

## WHY WE DO NOT REMEMBER

The loss of memory between incarnations and the failure to recall now any of our experiences previous to the present physical plane life has sometimes been cited as a negative kind of evidence against the hypothesis of rebirth. The point could not be made, however, by one who has studied the matter because careful scrutiny will show that the loss of memory is a necessary part of reincarnation. The fact that we do not remember is in perfect harmony with the principles of evolution. Indeed, the close student of the subject would be very much surprised if we could normally remember, because he does not get far until he sees, not only why we do not remember past incarnations but also why we should not remember them.

The very nature of the evolutionary work to be done by reincarnation necessitates a loss of memory on the material plane. Expression of consciousness through a physical body narrows its scope and thereby increases its efficiency. The cognition of the ego embraces a vast field, and includes past lives; but its limitation to a physical body, focuses the attention on the evolutionary work immediately in hand. The brain becomes the instrument of consciousness but also, fortunately, its limitation. If there were not loss of memory our minds would now range over the adventures of thousands of years in the past. It would encompass a vast drama with countless loves and hates, of many lives filled with pathos and tragedy. To thus distract the mind from the present life would retard our progress. When one is alone and in a secluded place one can think better and accomplish more than when in the midst of turbulent scenes and throngs of people. When there is less to think about the thinking is more effective. It is necessary to restrict the consciousness and limit the mind to the present life to get the most satisfactory results. The same truth is embodied in that old saying that whoever is jack of all trades is master of none. Concentration is necessary for progress. If we would master the lessons of this life we must not take other lives within the field of perception. The very process of reincarnation is a coming out of the general into the particular.

The permanent source of memory is, of course, in the causal body because it is that part of the mechanism of consciousness that does not perish when the work of a given incarnation is finished. Within it is stored all that has passed before the individual consciousness, but although memory of the past incarnations is there, it is not available to the physical consciousness at the present time. There will come a time in human evolution when memory of past lives will be the normal thing for the average person and then there will be no need of argument that we have lived here before, because everyone will remember it. The average human being is still far from that point and those who remember are few indeed; but those few are important witnesses. Those who personally know them, and know the remarkable purity, earnestness, usefulness and truthfulness of their lives, cannot but be very greatly impressed by their testimony.

Such evidence is valuable notwithstanding the fact that it is somewhat discounted in the minds of many who have met very ordinary people who confidently assert that they remember previous lives and declare themselves to have been great personages in the past. Sensible people will see at once that such claims are not so much evidence of past greatness as they are proof of present vanity. Some people do get glimpses of the past, but until they become trained observers in subtle matter there can be no absolute certainty of the accuracy of the fleeting visions, however honest the seer may be. That vanity is an important factor in some cases is evidenced by the fact that there are now living a number of women each of whom remembers that she was Mary, Queen of Scots!

Evolution means rising life after life to higher positions. It may not always be what the world would call advancement. It may be the change from ruler over a nation to a modest teacher of great truths; but that may be in reality a distinct advance. If those who so easily "remember" previous greatness would take second thought, they would see that it is not particularly creditable to be less now than one was in the past. In reincarnation we go forward, not backward, in intellect, power and influence. Nobody who grasps the evolutionary idea could possibly be pleased with a greater past and a lesser present. It would be more creditable to have been a menial then and something of an improvement now.

Those who really remember care the least about it and say the least about it. Old souls are modest souls. They are the personification of tranquil humility, a living evidence that true worth is modest and simple. Sometimes it probably does occur that one well along in evolution is drawn back into an obscure place in order that certain lacking qualities may be developed or opportunity for quiet and rapid progress may be fully utilized; but that is doubtless very rare and ordinarily a person with karmic associations such as a ruler must necessarily have, would not be found in a position of obscurity and in a narrow environment.

We should keep in mind the fact that our true and permanent life is in the causal body, and on the mental plane, and that there, alone, is unbroken memory possible, until we have reached a rather high point in evolution. The descent into matter in each incarnation is also beyond reach of the brain memory. Getting new bodies is the working out of natural law even as instinct works in animals. The whole animal kingdom, lacking the reasoning power of man, nevertheless adapts means to ends with unerring accuracy and with a precision that is beyond our comprehension. Even so is human evolution directed by impelling forces that are unknown to our waking consciousness; but our waking stage is only a small part of our consciousness—that fragment of it that can be expressed through the physical brain. The brain, being a limitation of consciousness, is therefore a limitation of memory, as certainly as a mountain range is a limitation of sight. In the higher realms we do know our wider life and vaster consciousness that includes the memory of our past incarnations, even as a traveler on the crest of a mountain range can see the winding trail by which he ascended; but when he descends into the valley the range behind him obscures the view. Only when he reaches the summit of the mountains next before him can he once more have unobstructed vision. Thus it is in the evolutionary journey of the soul. We are now in the valley of incarnation, and we are walled in by the physical brain—the limitation of our field of consciousness. Only when, between what we call death and our next incarnation, we have reached the heights of the causal level shall we be able to glance backward over our past lives; and when we come downward into another incarnation it will be as though we were descending in a narrow vale within mountain ranges that stand between us and the wider world.

Memory is dependent on things not within the control of the will. It often fails to establish facts which we wish to recall. We know, for example, the name of a certain person. There is no doubt that we know it and yet it is impossible to remember it at will. Tomorrow it will flash upon us, but we cannot remember it now, try as we may. If memory fails to produce its complete record even when we have a mental picture of just how that person looks, and know just where we have met him, it is certainly not remarkable that with no such immediate connection with our last incarnation we fail to recall it.

Our failure to remember a name we heard only a few hours ago is not because there is no inner record of it; for if there were no record there, we should never be able to recall it. Just as the failure to remember now what recently occurred does not prove that there is no record of the incident, so the failure to remember a former life does not prove that the record of our past incarnations is not within the imperishable causal body.

It may be asked why it is that, if we do not remember events that have occurred in past lives, and people we have known before, we do not now at least possess the technical knowledge previously familiar to us. What the soul gains from incarnation to incarnation is not concrete facts but something higher and far more valuable. It gains the essence of facts which gives the understanding of their true relationship; and this is the thing we call good judgment or common sense. A man does not succeed in business because he knows a lot of facts, but because he knows what to do with facts. Every theorist and dreamer is loaded with facts. The successful man is the one with balance and judgment.

It might seem on first thought that one who has been a carpenter in previous incarnations should have no need to learn the name and use of a saw, or one who has been a skillful penman to learn slowly to hold the pen and fashion the letters; but we must remember that the old soul is now "breaking in" a new physical instrument with which to express itself and that while it will be able to use all the skill it has previously evolved, its full expression must await the time when the new vehicle has been brought into responsive action.

The situation might be fairly illustrated by the case of a stenographer who is still using the original typewriter, in some remote corner of the earth, and who has not even seen or heard of any of the remarkable improvements made in such machines since their invention. If his old machine were suddenly taken away and a model of the present year were put in its place, it is obvious that he could at first make but little use of it—not because he has no skill but because he must become accustomed to the new machine before he can express himself through it. It would have mechanism and appliances that he could not immediately manage. That, however, has no relationship to abilities already acquired. All that he has previously evolved of skill and understanding, he possesses. He is as competent a typist as before the new machine arrived, but he must have a little time in which to adapt himself to the unaccustomed mechanism before he can freely express himself upon it. When that is accomplished, he will be more efficient than he was before because of the improved instrument he uses. Let us imagine also that the characters on the machine are in a foreign language which must be mastered before it can be used. Still the difficulties are not great enough for a fair illustration. We must also suppose that it is a living thing, with moods and emotions, and that it must pass through stages of growth comparable to infancy and youth. Under these handicaps it would be certain that the typist would appear to have very little knowledge and to possess little skill; yet as a matter of fact it is merely the conditions that temporarily prevent him from expressing his skill.

The gist of experience gained in the past represents skill that has no dependence whatever upon brain memory. If a man should suffer a lapse of memory, as sometimes happens, and wander about unable to give his name or place of residence, such loss of memory does not prevent his using any skill he may have evolved. If he is an athlete he may not know in what gymnasium he evolved his great strength, but he can use it just as effectively regardless of the absence of memory.

One who has been a skillful penman brings all his skill to the new incarnation but of course the new body must be trained to hold the pen and form the letters. Every teacher knows that one child will quickly learn that, and soon become a competent penman, while another can by no possibility exhibit skill in that particular art. The reason is that one has previously evolved his skill and the other has not, and may not, for several more incarnations.

It is sometimes objected that, by the hypothesis of reincarnation, we are required to go over the same ground again and again and learn what we have previously learned. But the criticism has no foundation in fact. There is undoubtedly some necessary recapitulation in the early part of the incarnation, just as there may be in the early part of a school term. But in the main we are thrown into new conditions which are calculated to develop additional faculties. We return to the same material plane but we find it with a higher form of civilization than when we were here before. Never before have we who are now here seen a civilization like this, with its age of steel and steam and electricity, with its marvelous opportunities for the development of the mechanical and scientific faculties in human nature. And that is another bit of evidence of the beauty and utility of the evolutionary scheme. We come back always to greater opportunities than we have yet known.

It is not only clear that the failure to remember the past has nothing to do with our ability to use the skill and wisdom we have previously evolved but it is equally obvious that it is the best of good fortune that we cannot remember the past. If we could do so that memory would keep alive the personal antagonisms of past incarnations. Nobody will deny that we have plenty of them in this incarnation or that the world would be the better if we could bury some of the present enmities in blank oblivion. If all quarreling neighbors were suddenly to lose memory of their feuds it would be an undeniable advantage to everybody concerned.

Nature's wisdom in veiling the past from us can be understood by observing the pernicious effects of remembering too long the blunders people make in this incarnation. Take the case of a very young man who has charge of his employer's money and who, finding himself pressed for ready cash, makes the grave mistake of "borrowing" a hundred dollars without his employer's knowledge and consent. The young man really believes he is borrowing it and knows just where the money is to come from to replace it soon, and he thinks nobody but himself will ever know anything about it; but to his consternation the money that was due him in a few days cannot be collected in time and an unexpected examination of his books leads to his arrest for embezzlement. He is convicted, sent to prison for a year and returns a marked man. Thoughtless society closes its doors against him. He seeks employment in vain. Nobody wants an ex-convict. He explains that he had no criminal intent; that he really was only guilty of youthful indiscretion and that he paid back the money later. But the world is too busy to listen. It sees only the court record, and that was against him. The public forgets, or never knows, the extenuating circumstances; but it never forgets two things—the verdict of guilty and the prison. The young man would almost give his life for a chance to wipe it all out, but it is impossible. It stands against him for life. Nature is wise. She does not permit our intolerance to extend injury too far. If we could remember from incarnation to incarnation, that man's misfortune might afflict him for thousands of years; but by the wise plan of closing all accounts at the end of each incarnation the mischief of remembering the blunders of others comes to an end. In the next incarnation all start with clear records again.

One of the objections that one sometimes hears against reincarnation is that it seems to separate us for long periods, if not forever, and that even when we meet those we have previously known and loved, there is no memory of the past. The answer to the first point is that the separation is wholly on the lower planes and that the time spent on the higher planes is many times that given to the lower. Separation is, of course, also unavoidable on the physical plane, even where people live together in the same house. The average man spends most of the day at his office and sleeps about eight hours during the twenty-four. He is really separated from his family most of the time during physical life; but there is no such separation on higher planes and there we spend by far the larger part of the entire period of evolution. The second point—that we do not now have the pleasure of knowing that our friends are those we knew and loved before—is not an important one. What is really important is that we again have them. If the ties of affection have been strong between us in the past there will be instant friendship when we meet for the first time in this incarnation. Those with strong heart ties are certain to be drawn into very close association life after life. It has been observed through the investigations that certain egos have been husband and wife, or parent and child, again and again. The renewal of such a close relationship depends upon the strength of the ties of affection; but if such a real bond between the souls is lacking the mere fact that they now are in the same family is no guarantee of such future intimate association. When two souls have strong ties arising out of past association the failure to remember that incarnation does not in the least weaken the ties; but it does mercifully hide the past contentions that are to be found in nearly all lives.

The failure to remember previous incarnations will be more clearly understood if we give some thought to the fact that the personality here on the material plane is only a fragment of the whole consciousness of the soul. As we come down into lower planes from the mental world each grosser grade of matter through which the ego expresses itself is an additional limitation of consciousness. On the astral plane each of us, whatever he may be here, is more alive and more keenly conscious. On the causal level of the mental plane he has enormously greater wisdom than here, with a still farther extension of consciousness that is quite beyond the present comprehension of the brain intelligence.

To put it differently the ego, as such, really does not come into incarnation at all. It merely sends outward a ray from itself—a mere fragment of itself, as a man might put his hand down into the water of a shallow stream to gather bits of ore from which gold can be obtained. So the ego puts a "hand," only down into denser matter to get the earthly experience that can be transmuted into the gold of wisdom and skill. That "hand" of the ego, that we know as the personality, gathers the experience and then it is withdrawn into the soul. During the incarnation the personality can be animated by only a little of the ego's vast intelligence and that is why it blunders so often. Veiled in dense matter, not much of the ego's consciousness can reach it.

The relationship between the ego and the personality may be illustrated by that which exists between the brain consciousness and that of the finger-tip. The difference, of course, is great. The finger-tip cannot see or hear or taste or smell. It is limited to one sense—touch. But that is a type of consciousness, and it can get experience and pass it on to the brain consciousness. A man may be addressing others and see some substance on the table beside him. It may be sand or salt. Without interrupting his lecture he can put down his finger and get at the truth about the matter. The finger-tip gets the information and passes it on to the brain consciousness. Meantime there has been no pause in the discourse. Not a phrase nor a word nor the shading of a thought has been missed. The intellectual life went on in its completeness while the ray of intelligence sent down in the finger-tip got and reported the fact as it was.

Just so the life of the ego—the true self of each of us—goes forward on its home plane while the personality here gropes for its harvest of experience. Some of those experiences will be painful to the personality, and the event will seem tragic here, but it will be a trifling event to the ego. In the illustration just used the substance on the table may prove to be neither sand nor salt, but tiny bits of glass.

Some of the sharp points may penetrate the finger and pain follows. To the finger-tip consciousness it is a blinding flash of distress that is overwhelming; but to the brain consciousness it is a trivial incident. And thus it is with our painful but very useful experiences here—illness, losses, accidents, separations, disasters, death—they often seem overwhelming to the physical consciousness, but to the ego they are but passing incidents.

The personality finishes its work and at death perishes, in the sense that it is drawn up and incorporated in the ego. Most people identify themselves so fully with the personality that its loss seems like a tragedy to them. But that feeling will trouble them no longer when the ego is understood to be the real self. We might say that the relationship between the ego and the personality is like that between man and child. Childhood perishes but only to be merged into manhood. When we look at that transformation from the viewpoint of the man it is quite satisfactory; but if looked at from the viewpoint of the child it may seem appalling. If one should say to one's son of three summers, "My child, the time will come when all these beautiful toys will be broken and lost and your little playmates will see you no more," it might cause much distress. It would seem to his limited child consciousness nothing less than a tragic destruction of all that makes life worth while; but when he reaches manhood he will look back with a smile to the trivial things of those early days. If there is something in his childhood of real, permanent value, it will persist in manhood. All the trivial and transient will have disappeared and he will be pleased that it is so, for manhood is the real life of the personality, as the ego is the real life, the soul.

As the memory of childhood lives in the brain of the man, so the memory of all the hundreds of incarnations persists in the causal body and becomes a possession of the ego. When we are sufficiently evolved to raise the consciousness to the level of the causal body, while still living on the physical plane, as some people are now able to do, we shall thus recover the memory of past lives. When that time comes, however, the soul is sufficiently advanced to use such wider knowledge without injury to others or to itself.

## CHAPTER XIII.

## VICARIOUS ATONEMENT

Back of the ancient doctrine of vicarious atonement is a profound and beautiful truth, but it has been degraded into a teaching that is as selfish as it is false. That natural truth is the sacrifice of the solar Logos, the Deity of our system. The sacrifice consists of limiting Himself in the matter of manifested worlds and it is reflected in the sacrifice of the Christ and other great teachers. Not the sacrifice of life but of voluntarily returning to live in the confinement of a material body. Nobody more than the Theosophist pays to the Christ the tribute of the most reverent gratitude; but he also holds with St. Paul that each must work out his own salvation. Were it not for such sacrifice the race would be very, very far below its present evolutionary level. The help that such great spiritual beings have given mankind is incalculable and is undoubtedly altogether beyond what we are able to comprehend. But to assume that such sacrifices relieve man from the necessity of developing his spiritual nature or in any degree nullify his personal responsibility for any evil he has done, is false and dangerous doctrine.

The belief in special creation arose in that period of our history when our ancestors knew little of nature. Modern science was then unborn and superstition filled the western world. Now that we do know much of the truths of nature, now that we know that creation is a continuous evolutionary process that is still going on, it is time to abandon the old conceptions and bring religious beliefs and scientific principles into harmonious relationship.

Wherever it touches the practical affairs of life the old idea of special creation and special salvation fails to satisfy our sense of justice and of consistency. Intuitively we know that any belief that is not in harmony with the facts of life is a wrong belief. The idea of special creation is not only inconsistent with the facts as science has found them, but it does not give us a sound basis for moral development.

The vital point against this plan of salvation is that it ignores the soul's personal responsibility and teaches that whatever the offenses against God and man have been, they may be cancelled by the simple process of believing that another suffered and died in order that those sins might be forgiven. It is the pernicious doctrine that wrongdoing by one can be set right by the sacrifice of another. It is simply astounding that such a belief could have survived the Middle Ages and should continue to find millions who accept it in these days of clearer thinking. But it seems that when people are taught a thing in childhood the mind accepts it then without reasoning and afterwards vaguely regards it as one of the established facts, without thinking farther about it. Upon reflection we see at once the impossibility of its being true. We hear of a lingering practice in a remote province of China, whereby a man convicted of a crime is permitted to hire a substitute to suffer the penalty in his stead. We laugh at that and know well enough that punishing the unfortunate substitute, who sacrifices himself to obtain a sum of money that will provide for his family, cannot regenerate the offender. Indeed, we see clearly that his willingness to shift the responsibility for his crime upon another only sinks him farther into iniquity.

By applying the principles involved in vicarious atonement to the events of daily life the absurdity of such a belief is the more readily seen. Let us suppose that that system of vicarious atonement for wrongdoing were to be adopted generally. Then every murderer who had the means would escape the consequences of his crime. Every burglar who was succesful enough to have the cash on hand could elude prison. Every pickpocket could hire a substitute to go to jail for him and thus continue his criminal career. Every embezzler would have the money to purchase freedom. Every successful thief could laugh at the law. It would make a mockery of justice. It would place a premium upon crime. However bad the dishonest might be it would make them worse. It would destroy the sense of personal responsibility, and personal responsibility is the basis of sound morals and the foundation of civilized society.

Yet that is precisely the sort of thing that goes with the belief in special creation and special **salva-**

tion—the teaching that we are not responsible for our sins and that by believing that another assumed them and died for us we can escape the results of our wrongdoing and thus be saved. What do we need to be saved from? From nothing but ourselves; from our selfishness, from our capacity to do evil, from our willingness to inflict pain, from our lack of sympathy with all suffering and from the heartlessness that is willing to let others suffer in order that we may escape. Salvation must necessarily mean capacity to enjoy heaven.. The man who is willing to purchase bliss by the agony of another is unfit for heaven and could not recognize it if he were there.

A heaven that is populated with those who see in vicarious atonement a happy arrangement for letting them in pleasantly and easily would not be worth having. It would be a realm of selfishness and that would be no heaven at all. A real heaven can be composed only of those who have eliminated selfishness; only of those who want to help others instead of trying to escape the consequences of their own acts; only of those who are manly and womanly and generous and just and true. Nothing less than a recognition of personal responsibility can lead to a heaven like that; yet the theory of vicarious atonement ignores it, waves it aside—in fact denies it!

Reincarnation represents personal responsibility and therefore justice. It shows that, not merely in the future, but also in this life, the degree of our happiness depends upon our past and present course. If that were generally understood it would necessarily promote morality. It furnishes a deterrent for the evil doer and a tremendous incentive for the man who desires to obey natural law and be happy. It shows the one that there is no possible way to avoid reaction; that he must return life after life to associations and environments determined by the ill he has done; that he can no more escape from the consequences of evil deeds than he can escape from himself; that he must ultimately suffer in turn the pain of every blow and the humiliation of every insult he is willing to inflict upon others. It assures the man of good intentions and right desires that every noble deed shall rise up in the future to bless him; that those whom he has helped shall become his helpers hereafter; that even his good intentions, that failed in their purpose through mistaken judgment, shall bring him joy in the future.

What a splendid thing it is to know that every right thought and act adds permanent value to the character; that all we learn in any life becomes an eternal possession; that we can add to the strength of our intellect, to our moral insight, to our compassion, to our wisdom, to our power, as certainly and definitely as a man can add to his bank account or permanent investments; that whatever we may be in this incarnation we can return again stronger and wiser and better!

The hypothesis of reincarnation shows our inherent divinity and the method by which the latent becomes the actual. Instead of the ignoble belief that we can fling our sins upon another it makes personal responsibility the keynote of life. It is the ethics of self-help. It is the moral code of self-reliance. It is the religion of self-respect!

Consider the utility as well as the common sense of a scheme of salvation that saves us because it evolves us; that never denies us a chance to rectify an error; that gives us an opportunity to right every wrong; that brings us back life after life until all enemies have been changed to friends; until all our latent powers have been evolved; until intellect has become genius; until sympathy has become compassion and the last moral battle has been fought and won.

## CHAPTER XIV.

## THE FORCES WE GENERATE

To say that life is a puzzle to most people is probably to state the best known fact in the world. Every thoughtful person has often paused in the rush and turmoil of daily affairs to ask himself what it is all about. If we look down from a tall building, into a busy street, at the endless stream of people flowing below, at the intricate swarm of human beings coming and going, and think of them only as related to this, it presents activity as meaningless as the movements of a community of ants. Nevertheless, the lack of purpose is merely apparent, not real. There is a reason why each is there and a reason will also determine his going. The seeming confusion exists only because we are unable to relate these people to the scenes through which they have moved before they appeared in the street. If we could do that, the chaos would disappear and we should see that reason and purpose govern the movements of each.

Just so it is with the life journey of every human being. As certainly as the street scene is but a fragment of a larger, orderly life, so is an incarnation, from infancy to old age, but a fragment of a soul's evolution, and what we call birth and death correspond to the appearance and disappearance of the people in the crowded street below us.

The fact that the coming and going in the street scene is not visibly related to something which preceded it, or to anything that shall follow it, proves that what we are observing is but a portion of some larger drama. We know that these people did not suddenly began to exist at the instant when we saw them and that they will not as suddenly cease to exist when they pass from our sight. We realize that they must have appeared in the street below us as the result of a train of causes and that when they disappear from our range of vision they will move through other scenes that must just as certainly be related to that fragment which we see.

If it were possible to extend our vision to include the entire life journey of each of the people in the street below, it would prove to be equally fragmentary. If we could trace the multitude from birth to death, we should find many things that we could not explain because they are not related to anything that has occurred during this life. We could find no satisfactory relationship between cause and effect. We should find that one is extremely selfish; that he cares nothing for the happiness of others; that he has no respect for the laws or usages of civil life; that he is both cruel and dishonest; yet he prospers amazingly and amasses great wealth. We should find that another had been crafty in business or politics, breaking promises and betraying friends, but that he had been successful in attaining fame and power. We should find that another had lived peacefully and piously all his life only to be murdered in his old age; that still another had killed several people but was never brought to justice for his crimes and finally died peacefully surrounded by his friends. We should find that many learned but little from their experiences and that, after a long life, they departed not much wiser than when they came. In many others we should find rapid mental and moral growth while multiplied thousands died in infancy before they had time to gain any experience and with no apparent reason for being here at all. We should find that many wrongs are not righted and that many good harvests are not reaped. We should see, in short, that doing justice does not always insure justice; that being kind does not guarantee an immediate return of kindness; that being patient does not save us from the irritable; that being honest is no security against loss by thieves, and that living in peace does not always protect us from violence.

Thus life, as we look upon it in a single incarnation, is a mystery and apparently a contradiction. It seems to defy law and to disregard consistency; but since there must necessarily be a cause for every effect, we are forced to the conclusion that some unknown law is at work which, when understood, will enable us to reduce the apparent confusion to order. That law is the law of action and reaction which, in time, inexorably works out the destiny of every human being. To that law we may appeal and build character as we admire it; with that law we may shape destiny as we would have it.

We should carefully study the laws of life for the same reason that a ship should carry a compass.

Most people are merely adrift upon a shoreless sea. No chart marks a destination, no rudder holds a course. They are at the mercy of every adverse wind that blows, and if they have made a little progress when night comes at the end of life's journey it is because they have been borne onward by the ceaseless tide of evolution, and not because they have resolutely grasped the opportunities for a fair and prosperous voyage that lie within reach of every human being. In order that we may avoid this aimless drifting, with its wasted energy and its painful collisions, we must know something of the principles that govern the journey—something of that great occult law of cause and effect under whose operation our existence can be a life of misery and gloom and disaster, or a life of light and love and joy.

The first step toward a satisfactory life is to recognize the fact that natural law governs everywhere, and precisely as much in the realm of morals as in the world of physical affairs. As we pass through life we have various experiences, establish a certain relationship with the other human beings we meet, contract certain obligations and responsibilities, do or fail to do certain things, and thus set up a train of causes that must somewhere, at some time, work out into certain definite results. It is a truth of nature that no force can be lost; that no particle of energy can be put forth anywhere in the universe without a natural result following. If you toss a pebble in the air the act is not complete when the stone leaves your hand. A result must follow. Under the operation of what we call the law of grav-

## The Forces We Generate

ity the pebble must return to the earth. When you wind a clock the energy you generate must likewise have its result but not so immediately. It drives the mechanism of the clock for a certain definite period. The result is somewhat delayed, but it must be an exact and complete working out of the cause.

This law of action and reaction applies to every putting forth of energy by a human being. Each thought and emotion and act is a disturbance in some degree of nature's equilibrium and it will readjust itself as certainly as the rivers flow to the sea. Sometimes it expresses itself immediately, as in the case of the pebble. In more complex matters it is delayed, as in the instance of the clock; but sometime, somewhere, it must exactly work itself out. No human being can escape the consequences of his lightest thought or slightest deed. We must reap precisely as we sow. No evasion is possible. Death does not settle the score any more than moving to a new town will pay debts in the old one.

In all the universe there can be no such thing as chance. Nothing merely happens. Every thought, every movement, every expenditure of energy, is governed by natural law. Every cause must have a certain definite effect, modified, of course, by all subsidiary causes. There is no such thing as luck, good or bad. Back of every piece of good fortune lies the cause that we ourselves have somewhere created, perhaps unconsciously, perhaps in a previous life. Behind every particle of ill fortune likewise lies the energy that we ourselves have generated. We make our own sunshine and shadow, health and disease, friends and foes, heaven and hell; and since a man really reaps as he sows he has only himself to blame if the harvest is thistles instead of figs. It at once becomes clear that misfortune can no longer be called "the visitation of God," nor can responsibility for evil deeds be conveniently charged to Satan. It makes a man just what every manly man desires to be—a self-reliant being with neither the power nor the desire to escape responsibility.

To have convincing proof that in the long run we reap as we sow, we need only carefully observe the people about us. We see that they are doing this so far as causes *can* work out in one life. We know that the man who hates people is universally disliked; that the person who has a good word for all is himself considerately treated; that the fighter is a target for others' vengeance while the man of peace is usually free from assault. We see that the thief loses more than he steals, for he is deprived of his plunder and loses his liberty besides; while the philanthropist does not grow poor. We know that the pleasant are sought and the selfish are shunned; that the tolerant are considered and that the narrow go unheard; that peacemakers usually have peace and that killers are killed. We reap as we sow.

We are, then, determining in this life largely what kind of treatment we shall receive in the days to come, and we are also creating the causes that shall make our future lives pleasant or painful. The subject is one of the most complex with which Theosophy deals, but occult investigators carefully watching the working out of this law of cause and effect have observed some unvarying results. One of these is that whoever in one life faithfully discharges his duties and utilizes the opportunities that come to him, always finds a still wider opportunity awaiting him. There is said to be no kind of exception to this rule. On the other hand, neglected opportunity is followed by loss of future opportunity. And why not? Nature does nothing uselessly.

That thought and desire are forces as certainly as electricity is, the student of the occult knows, but the world is not quite yet at the point where the fact is generally accepted. When Franklin began his experiments with electrical force almost nobody believed there was any such thing in existence; yet today we use it to carry our messages, to run our trains and to drive our machinery. Had anybody predicted all that, at the time of the first experiments, he would have been considered rash indeed. What the world accepts or rejects at any particular time usually has little relationship to the facts. The general public can be expected to come trailing along, about a half century late, with its acceptance and approval of the truth.

Thought is a force or telepathy and hypnotism would be impossible. In telepathy two human brains work somewhat as two instruments in wireless telegraphy do. It is no more wonderful in the one case than in the other. In wireless telegraphy the communication is through the vibratory waves in imponderable matter, which we know freely interpenetrate solids. In telepathy the process is much the same, except that the vibratory waves are in a still rarer grade of matter. Thought-force, working in this impalpable matter, just as electricity works through the intangible ether, molds it into various forms. These thought-forms act upon others and react upon the person who generates them. Thus we are establishing an invisible relationship between ourselves and other people and with material things, which must and will produce certain exact results that will make or mar our fortunes far into the future.

When we think, we create a thing—a thought-form. It persists for a length of time in proportion to the intensity of the thought. It gets renewed vitality from each repetition of the thought. It reacts upon the mind that produced it, giving further impulses to that kind of thinking. If a man thinks of a person in a particular way, let us say with hatred, he creates a certain kind of thought-form. If he constantly gives it new life by continued thinking about it, that thought-form becomes strongly vitalized and grows in power. It reacts upon him, stimulating his mind to fresh thoughts of hatred. If the object of his wrath is similarly thinking hatred of him it presently grows into a feud, an encounter, perhaps a murder; for he has generated an evil force of great power which must produce its result as certainly as does the thunderbolt.

Sometimes we hear of an impulsive crime. One man suddenly slays another, and a close examination of all the circumstances reveals no provocation at all commensurate with the deed. The murderer himself is bewildered and unable to comprehend just how it occurred. He can only say that he struck the fatal blow before he fully realized what he was doing. This statement may be the truth and yet not lessen his responsibility; for when he has thought and thought of doing this thing, when he has intensely desired to do it, and is then suddenly confronted with the opportunity, he may be automatically hurried into it; *for an act is but the outward expression of an inner condition.* This man is already a murderer in the realm of the mind. The motive is fully developed. The desire to take life is matured. He is restrained only by fear of consequences to himself—a fear that may be momentarily pushed aside by anger. Deep within his soul the murder is already committed. On the stage of his imagination the tragedy has been played again and again. He has experienced the secret joy of cunningly entrapping his victim. He has felt the fury of anger as he overpowered his enemy. With the gloating exultation of vengeance achieved, he has, in imagination, plunged the knife into his heart and felt no pang of pity. The moral ignoramus—for that he is, regardless of his intellectual development— has brooded in malice until the accumulated force of hatred hurried him into the crime the instant he was confronted by the circumstances that made its commission possible.

Thought-force, like all force, may be used for a good or a bad purpose, just as electricity may be used to light a city or to destroy a human life. If we turn this thought-force in the opposite direction it is equally potent for good. If we think kindly of people we shall, in time, have no enemies. If we encourage noble thoughts we shall soon find ourselves lifted into a higher moral atmosphere. We shall find it becoming easier and easier to think nobly, to act generously, to deal justly. We shall find our friends increasing, our vexations disappearing and our pleasure in life growing constantly keener.

We get back from the world what we give to it. If one throws a ball against the wall it rebounds, and with a force proportional to the original energy that propelled it. A blow is invariably met with a blow and a smile with a smile. If we observe people studiously we shall see that they are daily reaping rewards and incurring penalties as a result of the mental and emotional forces they have generated.

There is something almost startling in the immutability of all natural laws and their utterly impersonal aspect. They are the operation of forces which, in themselves, are not related to what 'we call good and bad. The law of gravity will illustrate the point. It operates with no consideration whatever for character or motives. It holds all people, good and bad alike, firmly upon the earth while it whirls through space. If a saint and a fiend stumble over a precipice, it will hurl them both to the bottom with perfect impartiality. If the fiend, who may just have murdered a victim, is more cautious than the saint and avoids the precipice, the law has not favored him. He has merely reaped the reward of his alertness in spite of his bad morals. The saintly man may have come from some deed of mercy but the law of gravity takes no account of that. When he stepped over the precipice, and was dashed to death, he paid the penalty of carelessness regardless of his benevolence. But this immutability of natural law is not in the least terrifying when we look closely at it. On the contrary it is within that very immutability that divine beneficence and compassion are hidden. It is only by the constancy of the changeless law that we can calculate with absolute certainty and surely attain the results at which we aim.

Why should there be such a law operating in the mental and moral realm? Because only thus can we evolve. We must not only change from ignorance to wisdom but from selfishness to compassion, from wrongdoing to perfect harmlessness. How would that be possible without the law of cause and effect, without action and reaction which brings, sooner or later, pleasure for righteousness and pain for evil deeds? Only under such a law can we learn what is the right and what is the wrong thing to do. If it is agreed that we are souls, that evolution is a fact, and that perfection is the goal of the human race, then the necessity for the law of action and reaction is as obvious as the reason for a law of gravity.

Every human being is constantly generating forces, and they are not only factors in determining the kind of life he will lead here, the degree of success or failure that will characterize it, and the state of his consciousness on inner planes after the death of the physical body, but also the environment and the relationships he will return to in the following incarnation.

All people are constantly thinking and desiring

and, with varying degrees of energy, are putting thought and desire into action. These forces sent out into the realms of thought, emotion and activity, produce definite reactions, or consequences, and to them the man is bound until justice is done and the soul has learned its evolutionary lesson.

Desires generate a kind of energy that plays a most important role in the drama of human evolution. The law operates to bring together the desirer and the object that aroused the desire; for the soul can judge the wisdom of its desires by observing the result of gratifying them. Thus do we acquire discrimination. It is usually a strong desire nature that brings trouble of various kinds and yet the force of desire it is that pushes all evolution onward. Through experience the soul finally learns to control desire, to raise lower desires into higher ones and thus ultimately to attain non-attachment and liberation.

Actions are the physical expression of thoughts and desires and, as we are constantly simultaneously thinking, desiring and acting, very complex results arise. In the multitudinous activities of life we set up relationships with other souls, some of the results of which reach far into the future. The average man, with no knowledge of the laws under which he is evolving, is usually making both friends and foes for future incarnations as well as for the present one, and is often unwittingly laying up pain and sorrow for himself which a little occult knowledge would enable him to avoid. Every injury that he inflicts will return to him, though not necessarily in kind. Nature does not punish. She merely teaches. Her great concern seems to be that all souls shall get on in evolution and when a lesson is learned her purpose is accomplished.

It is a generally acknowledged fact that we must all reap as we sow. But the people who assent to that truth often have in mind very different beliefs about it. Many believe that in some way we shall suffer in a future state for the wrong we have done here. The Theosophist has a very definite idea. He believes that each act has a reaction which exactly corresponds to its cause; that every thought and emotion reproduce their kind as certainly as the seed of a plant reproduces its kind, and no other; that all the incarnations of the soul are thus knit together in a great series of causes and effects and that these have the same definite relationship that exists between the course a young man follows and the results of that course in his latter days. If he is kind and helpful in early life, he will have many friends in later life, but if, in his earlier years, he makes enemies of everybody and does nothing to set such blunders right, he will certainly be friendless in his old age.

People speak of a judgment day that is to come. To the Theosophist every day is a judgment day and the working of natural law brings the penalty or the reward. The judgment day for the sharp censure of another's mistake comes when somebody exposes a blunder that we have made. The judgment day for a drunken bully who runs amuck on the street comes when a policeman clubs him into submission. The judgment day for the soul that cruelly maimed another's body comes when he is reborn with a defective brain and the awful blight of idiocy falls upon him. Such things are not punishments but merely reactions, and to the clear comprehension of the soul who looks back upon the distant cause of the affliction with unclouded vision, a necessary lesson is taught by the sad experience.

The forces we generate in each incarnation not only modify that one but shape and determine the next and succeeding ones. Our friends, our families, our business associates, our nation, are determined by what we have thought and felt and done in the past and by the lessons it is necessary for us to learn. Our wealth or poverty, our fame or obscurity, our strength or frailty, our intelligence or stupidity, our good or bad environment, our freedom or limitations, all grow out of the thoughts and emotions and acts of the past. From their consequences there is no possibility of escape; but that does not mean that we are the helpless slaves of a fate from which there is no release.

It is sometimes said by those who have misunderstood, that the theosophical hypothesis is identical with fatalism. No assertion could be more erroneous. The conception of fatalism is that the universe is a huge machine set running by some infinite being who ordered its intricate movements an eternity in advance, with the fate of all men fixed and inflexible like cogs; that, try as he may, a man can be nothing but what he was destined by this infinite being to be and that regardless of the man's apathy and indifference he will be that anyhow. If such a belief were universal, it would put an end to human progress by leaving us with no incentive.

The theosophical conception is just the reverse of that. It holds that men are literally gods in the making; that each has within him potentially all the attributes of deity; that these are being slowly developed by the process of evolution; that among other things he is evolving will-power; and that man where he stands now is not the result of either his environment or his will, but of evolutionary forces, and that important factors in his development are his will, plus his environment, acting and reacting upon each other. It holds that man is moving forward with accelerating speed and the very gist of the idea is that the rapidity of his evolution depends upon his own efforts. So, as a matter of fact, the theosophical hypothesis is precisely the opposite of fatalism.

It may be thought that if our present conditions are the result of our past thoughts, emotions, and acts, these conditions must be just, and that we should not, therefore, seek to change them. If one's neighbor is in the depths of poverty and has bad health it might be argued that that is his just fate and that no one has a right to interfere; but such a view is in error because it leaves oneself out of the problem as one who might stand aside and look at the universe. The universe is all-inclusive and the prosperous man is as much a factor in the problem as his poverty-stricken neighbor. If the poverty and ignorance and apathy of the world are needed factors in human development, equally so are the strength and knowledge and altruism.

While unfortunate conditions, either of the individual or of whole classes, are just the circumstances that must inevitably have resulted from the sum total of past causes, and are also the conditions required to teach the necessary lesson to those individuals, classes or nations, yet when these conditions have accomplished the purpose of awakening the desire for better things, they have done their work and should be transcended. Therefore, while our present environment, physical, social, and moral, is of our own making, the moment we realize that it is susceptible of improvement, the instant we are able to see a higher ideal, it is our duty to seek and to insist upon that improvement to the limit of our ability.

Those who are interested in the long-time discussion over free-will and determinism have often been impressed with the remarkably strong arguments that can be marshaled by each side to the controversy. Either side, when presented alone, appears to be conclusive. The explanation lies in the fact that each *is* right, but only to a certain point. Both free will and necessity are factors and when the theosophical viewpoint is understood the apparent contradiction disappears. We are temporarily bound, *but we did the binding*, by the desires we indulged in and the emotions we freely harbored in the past.

The condition of temporary restraint in which we now find ourselves may be likened to that of a party of gold hunters who go into the interior of the

Klondike to locate mines. They are all aware that in that remote northern country navigation closes very early and that after the last boat leaves there is no possibility of getting out of that region until navigation opens again in the next season.* Some of them are discreet and reach the landing in ample time. Others are careless. They continue their search for gold a little too long, allowing barely time for the return trip. Then the unexpected happens; a sudden storm, a swollen river that cannot be crossed and they arrive at the steamer landing a day too late. The boat has sailed and they must become prisoners of the ice king. It's a great misfortune but they alone are responsible. They cannot escape from the Klondike for many months but while there they are absolutely free. They can build a cabin and either waste the time with idle games or seriously think and study. They are limited, but free within the limitation, which was of their own making. It is precisely so with us in the environment of the present incarnation and with our various fortunes. We made them and, when the forces with which we did it are exhausted, we shall be free. Meantime we can do much toward modification and improvement. We have such a degree of will power as we have evolved and we can use it within the self-imposed limitations that afflict us.

The reactions from the forces we generate naturally do us exact justice simply because they *are* reactions. We reap in the long run precisely what we sow. The reaction may sometimes seem harsh but consideration of the matter from all points of

---
*Editor's note. True at the time this book was written.

view will show that mercy as well as justice is a factor. Let us consider the method by which nature changes recklessness into caution. A man is careless, we will say, about lighting a cigar and throwing the burning match down wherever it may fall. He may go on doing that for a long time with no serious result, yet all careful people know that he is a source of danger. Some time ago a newspaper told the story of such a man, who passed along the street, lighted a cigarette and carelessly flung the flaming match from him. A nurse was passing with her tiny charge in its carriage. The match fell on some of the light, airy wraps of the infant and they burst into a blaze. Before the fire could be extinguished the child was so badly burned that it died the next day. In such a tragedy the law of adjustment has brought two blundering souls together. One is reaping the reaction from his recklessness in a previous incarnation and the other is imperiling his future by his present carelessness.

The moment such a case is stated we realize the necessity for something that will cure the latter of such fatal carelessness. He is a menace to the people and property in his vicinity. No law, however, can be invoked. He had no criminal intent but he is none the less dangerous, as the incident proved. We are helpless, however, to prevent his continued carelessness; but nature is not helpless. Under the law of action and reaction he must reap as he has sown. It may be in the latter part of this incarnation, or it may be in the following one, but sooner or later his carelessness will react and he will lose his physical body in pain and distress and come to know personally just what his recklessness means. In the reaction, a part only of which is on the physical plane, he gets the experience that is necessary to set him right. The folly of his course is so driven in on his consciousness that he is changed from the careless man to the careful man.

In such a tragedy there is no injustice. This heedless soul can learn his lesson only through experience and the sooner he gets that experience the better it will be, both for him and for others—the better for others because it removes a source of danger to them, and better for him because the longer he remains the careless man the longer will painful reactions continue. Nature is both just and merciful. In truth, not nature, but one's own self is the actor. No power outside ourselves ever inflicts a penalty upon us. There are really neither rewards nor punishments. There are merely consequences. If an infant picks up a live coal, it will be burned. It is innocent and ignorant, but that will not prevent the operation of natural law. It must suffer the consequence of the mistake. At first thought that seems cruel, but upon reflection we see that in no other way can its life be made safe from fire; and the pain of a burnt finger is as nothing compared to the value of the lesson learned. Following this method of teaching by experience, nature is constantly permitting us to suffer the minimum of pain in order to escape the maximum of disaster.

It is a legal maxim that ignorance of the law excuses no man. This may sometimes work an apparent hardship, but there is no other way in which society can be protected—no other way to secure the greatest good to the greatest number. If we ignorantly violate law, either statutory or natural, we must suffer for it. Ignorance is the cause of all suffering. Happiness is attained through wisdom.

It may be thought that if a misfortune comes to us as the result of our wrong thinking and acting in a past life we can now know nothing of its cause and therefore we cannot profit by the reaction. Every cause must work out its natural effect regardless of our memory about it. We may do an indiscreet thing in youth and still suffer for it in old age, long after we have apparently learned our lesson and perhaps after we have forgotten its origin. Even so do the effects from one life reach into the next. There is another point to be remembered. While we are not conscious in the physical brain of the past errors for which we are now unwillingly paying the penalties, the higher self, the soul, does remember.

When we have advanced in evolution to the point where we can bring the memories of past lives into the present one—as all of us shall ultimately do—we can trace remote causes into present effects. Meantime nothing is being lost, for the result of the slightest experience is stored in the invisible self, and it becomes available to us in proportion that we open the channel to that higher consciousness.

The thing we call conscience is but the impulse from the higher self. It is the soul memory of past experience coming through in the form of impressions about a certain thing being right or wrong. If we have had painful experience about it we get the warning impression to avoid that line of action. If we have not had experience through action or observation, or have not had enough of it to teach the lesson fully, we get no warning and go ahead, led by desire, until we do learn. None of us have any doubt about this dual nature of man for it is a matter of daily experience. We note the constant warfare between the spiritual and material, the higher and lower. The lower grovels, the higher soars—a ceaseless conflict between the animal and the spiritual, desire continually plunging downward in pursuit of the material attractions but warned and checked by conscience.

There are two impressive points here involved. One is that under the operation of natural law, causes must work out into results regardless of memory, and the other is that, although we may not be conscious of the fact in the physical brain, the lesson is absorbed by the higher consciousness and will guide us in the future.

The principles of justice are never violated in teaching the soul its evolutionary lessons. Nothing can come to a man that he does not merit and that which often looks like a misfortune is only the beneficent working of the law seen from an angle that makes it illusory. It may be thought that it is scarcely "beneficent working of the law" when some disaster occurs. Sometimes a theatre is burned and scores of people, including children, lose their lives. How can Theosophy explain that?

How can it be explained by those who hold that

the soul is created at birth? If God really brings the soul into its original expression in an infant body, why does He throw it out again in a few years, or even months? What can be the purpose? It would be difficult indeed to explain the death of children if the soul were created at birth. But let us look at it from the theosophical viewpoint. The child is an old soul with a young body. Hark back to the case of the man whose carelessness caused the death of the baby in its carriage. He, and others like him, are again in incarnation and in the burning theatre they get the reaction of the unfortunate forces they have generated. But why so many in some catastrophes? it may be asked. A principle is not affected by the number involved. If we can see justice in the death of one person we can see justice in the death of a hundred. It is simply class instruction. People of a kind have been drawn together.

We should not forget that we see only a small fragment of any such matter from the physical plane. We form an opinion, however, on that inadequate survey and are quick to declare our estimate of the justice or injustice involved. But our verdict depends wholly upon a viewpoint. Let us suppose, for example, that a man strolls down the street and that, as he turns a corner, he suddenly comes upon a little tragedy of life. A young man is lying on the ground while two others are assaulting him. The sympathies of the average man would assuredly be with the man on the ground. Now, let us suppose that the observer had been a moment earlier. He would then have been in time to have turned the corner with the two assailants and would have seen the young man, who is now being assaulted, rush upon a defenseless woman, push her down, snatch her purse and dash away but, fortunately, in the direction of the men who were just coming upon the scene. Had our observer seen the entire affair he would have reversed his opinion and said that the thief got what he deserved. Thus it is in our inadequate physical plane view of what we call a calamity. It may appear to involve an injustice, but only because we do not see the entire transaction. Sometimes those who admit the operation of this law in the present life, where we know cause and effect may be separated by many years, ask why it should apply to future incarnations, granting for the moment that they agree that there are future lives to be lived here. We can easily see how our acts during one day have a determining effect on our affairs the next day. If we neglect business, if we fail to keep engagements, we know that unfavorable results must follow. A night during which we forget it all has intervened but that does not in the least save us from the results of the causes we generated the day before. Just so do the thoughts and acts of one incarnation affect the following ones whether we remember or not.

There is nothing fantastic about the idea that a cause created in one incarnation works out into an effect in a succeeding incarnation. The long period between cause and effect and the fact that the persons concerned have no continuous knowledge of the matter do not affect the principle involved.

The "memory of nature" is not merely a poetic name. It is a phrase that designates a part of the marvelously complex mechanism by which human evolution is accomplished. In the earlier history of physical science such a term would have been meaningless; but in the light of more recent discoveries, there is nothing startling in the idea. Our conceptions of matter have been revolutionized in recent years. We have learned that even in its grosser grades, it is enormously more impressionable than had been supposed—a thing of which the mellowing of wood in a violin under the vibrations of musical notes ought to have given us an earlier hint. The sensitiveness of the ether which permits wireless communications at great distances gives some suggestion of the degree to which the responsiveness of matter must rise on higher planes than this. If, in addition, we take into account the work of the superintending intelligences to be dealt with in the following chapter, we have in toto a plan of human evolution in which each of us is indeed his own recorder of thought, emotion, motive and act—not a mere record as a book is written, but a series of activities which continue their being in living matter and bind him to the forces he has generated; and which must, whether instantly or very remotely, react upon him in minutest exactitude.

Those who study the occult laws that shape human destiny may learn to use them for their rapid progress and for insuring a comfortable, as well as a spiritually profitable, life journey; but before we can work successfully within the law we must know that the law really exists. Most people seem either to believe there is no law that will certainly bring them the results of their evil thoughts and acts or that, if there is such a law, they can in some way elude it and escape the consequences of its violation; and so we see them pass through life always doing the selfish thing or the thoughtless thing. They falsify facts, they harbor evil thoughts, they engage in gossip, they have their enemies and hate them, they scheme to bring discomfort and humiliation upon those whom they dislike. And then, when the harvest from this misdirected energy is ripe and they are misled by the falsehoods of others to their loss and injury, when they fall into the company of cheats and are swindled, when a false story is started about them, when—through no fault of the moment —they are plunged into grief, they merely call it so much bad luck and go blindly on with their generation of wrong forces that will, in due time, bring them another enforced reaping of pain.

The existence and operation of this law of cause and effect are set forth repeatedly in the Christian scriptures. "With what measure ye mete it to others it shall be measured to you," is certainly explicit. In Proverbs* we have this definite declaration: "Whoso diggeth a pit shall fall therein, and he that rolleth a stone, it shall return upon him." Of course the language is figurative. No writer of common sense would assert that every time a workman digs a pit he shall tumble into it nor that whenever any-

---

* *Proverbs, XXVI, 27.*

body rolls a stone it will roll back upon him! We dig pits in the moral world whenever we injure another with a false story, whether we originate it or merely repeat it, and into such a pit we shall ourselves fall, in the reaction of the law. We loosen and set rolling the stones of envy and hatred and they shall return to crush us down to failure and humiliation in the reactions that follow. We have ignorantly generated evil forces under the law when we could have used it for our success and happiness.

"Judge not, that ye be not judged," is another statement of the law of action and reaction. It is not an assertion that we should not judge because we are not qualified nor because we may ignorantly wrong another with such judgment. It is an explicit statement that the consequence of judging others is that we, in turn, shall be judged. If we criticize, we shall be criticized. If we condemn others for their faults and failures, we shall be condemned. If we are broad and tolerant and remain silent about the frailties of others we shall be tolerantly regarded.

All of us who have studied the subject find in our daily lives the evidence of the truth of such Biblical declarations. We know perfectly well that anger provokes anger and that conciliation wins concessions, while retaliation keeps a feud alive. We know that retort calls out retort, while silence restores the peace. In all little things it is usually within the power of either party to the trouble to have peace instead of turmoil—it is just a matter of self control. But in the larger events it is not always so. They are not invariably within our immediate

## The Forces We Generate

control because they are often the results of causes generated in the past which we can no longer modify; and this brings us to a wider view of this law of cause and effect.

If we look at the life history of an individual as it stretches out from birth to death it presents a remarkable record of events that appear to have no logical relationship to each other. In childhood, there may have been either great happiness or great sorrow and suffering regardless of character qualities, and there is nothing in the present life of the child to explain either. The child itself may be gentle and affectionate and yet it may be the recipient of gross abuse and cruel misunderstanding. In maturity we may find still greater mysteries. Almost invariably there are mingled successes and failures, pleasures and pains; but when we come to analyze them we fail to find a satisfactory reason for them. We see that the successes often arrive when they are not warranted by anything that was done to win them, and for the want of any rational explanation we call it "good luck." We also observe that sometimes failure after failure comes when the man is not only doing his very best but when all of his plans will stand the test of sound business procedure. Baffled again we throw logic to the winds and call it "bad luck."

"Luck" is a word we use to conceal our ignorance and our inability to trace the working of the law. Suppose we were to ask a savage to explain how it is that a few minutes' time with the morning paper enables one to know what happened yesterday in a city on the opposite side of the earth. He knows nothing of reports and cables and presses. He cannot explain it. He cannot even comprehend it. But if he is a vain savage and does not wish to admit his ignorance he might solemnly assert that the reason we know is because we are lucky; and he would be using the word just as sensibly as we use it!

If by luck we mean chance, there is no such thing in this world. Chance necessarily means chaos and the absence of law. From the magnificent, orderly procession of hundreds of millions of suns and their world systems that wheel majestically through space down to the very atom, with its mysterious electrons, the universe is a stupendous proclamation of the all-pervading presence of law. It is a mighty panorama of cause and effect. There is no such thing as chance.

What then *is* good luck? We know that people do receive benefits which they apparently have not earned yet there cannot be a result without a cause. They have earned it in other lives when the conditions did not permit immediate harvesting of the results of the good forces generated and nature is paying the debt and making the balance of her books at this period. It may be in the case of one that some specific act is attracting its reward, or it may be in the case of another that he is nearing the point of evolution where he no longer desires things for himself, only to discover that nature fairly flings her treasures at his feet. He has put himself in harmony with evolutionary law—with the divine plan, and nothing which he needs is withheld. With the in-

## The Forces We Generate

sight of genius Ella Wheeler Wilcox stated the law in eight lines:

> Luck is the tuning of our inmost thought
> To chord with God's great plan. That done, ah know
> Thy silent wishes to results shall grow,
> And day by day shall miracles be wrought!
> Once let thy inner being selflessly be brought
> To chime with universal good, and lo!
> What music from the spheres shall through thee flow,
> What benefits shall come to thee unsought!

When we eliminate chance, then, we are forced to seek the cause of unexplained good or bad fortune beyond the boundaries of this life because there is nothing else we can do. We have results to explain and we know they do not come from causes that belong to this incarnation. They must of necessity arise from causes belonging to a past life.

The moment we get away from the narrow view that we began existence when we were born, most of the mysteries about us disappear and we can invoke natural law and logically explain everything. Why does one person begin life with a good mind while another is born with small mental capacity? Because one worked hard at life's problems in past incarnations while the other led a butterfly existence and merely amused himself. Why does one move serenely through trying circumstances always maintaining a cheerful view of life while another loses control of his temper at the slightest annoyance and wears himself out with trifling vexations? Only because one has for a long period practiced self-control while the other has never given a thought to the matter. Why is one so thoughtful of others that he wins universal love and admiration while another is so self-centered that he makes no true friends at all? Again past experience explains it. The one has studied the laws of destiny and lived by them while the other has not yet even learned of their existence.

If we put aside the old belief that the soul is created at birth, and keep in mind the more scientific view that we have all lived many lives before, we shall no longer be puzzled because we find in a man's life some good fortune when he has apparently done nothing to deserve it, for we see that he must, in a previous life, have set in motion the forces which now culminate in this result. We are no longer mystified when apparently causeless misfortunes befall him for we know that in the nature of things he did generate the causes in the past. A single incarnation has the same relation to the whole of the soul's evolution that a single day has to one lifetime. As the days are separated by the nights and yet all the days are related by the acts which run through them, from childhood to old age, so the incarnations are separated by periods of rest in the heaven world and yet all the incarnations are related by the thoughts and acts that bind them together. What we did yesterday modifies the events of today, and what we did in our last incarnation is affecting the present life. The one fact is no more remarkable than the other. As we mould old age by youth so we are shaping the coming incarnation by this one. Before we shall be able to see the utter reasonableness of the truth that what we are now is the result of our past we must have a clear understanding of the relationship between the soul and the body. The physical body in each incarnation is the material expression of the soul—of what it has come to be at that stage of its evolution, of its moral power or weakness, of its wisdom or ignorance, of its purity or its grossness. One's face is, at each moment, the tangible expression of one's thought. Every change of consciousness registers itself in matter. A man has emotions. He feels a thrill of joy and his face proclaims the fact. He becomes angry, and the change from joy to anger is registered in physical matter so that all who can see his face are aware of the change in his consciousness, which they cannot see. These are passing changes like sunshine and shadow and they are obvious to all; but we know that, as the years pass, the constant influence of consciousness moulds even physical matter into more permanent form. A soul of sunny disposition finally comes to have benevolent features while one of morose tendency as certainly has a face of settled gloom. Nobody can contact the soul of another with any physical sense we possess yet nobody has the slightest doubt of his ability to distinguish between a sunny, peaceful soul and a soul that is not in harmony with life. We know the difference only because consciousness moulds matter. Consciousness is continually influencing matter and the major part of its work is not visible to us. What the consciousness is, the body gradually becomes. Whether we are now brilliant or stupid, comely or deformed, is the result of the activities of consciousness, in this and previous lives.

Consider a specific thing like deformity. We can readily understand one of the causes that may have brought it about. If in a past life a person was guilty of deliberate cruelty to another, and on account of it suffered great mental and emotional distress afterward, it would be no remarkable thing if the mental images of the injuries inflicted on his victim are reproduced in himself. In idiocy we have apparently merely a distorted brain so that the soul cannot function freely through it. Might not that distortion of the physical brain easily be the result of violent emotional reaction from cruelties in a past life? The soul that can be guilty of cruelty is seeing things in distorted fashion—out of proportion. This distortion of consciousness must register a corresponding distortion in matter, for the body is the faithful and accurate reflection of that consciousness. It is precisely because the body is the true and exact expression of the consciousness in physical matter that the palmist and phrenologist can sometimes give us such remarkable delineations of character. The record is there in hand and head for those who are clever enough to read it accurately.

This broader outlook on the life journey, extending over a very long series of incarnations, gives us a wholly different view of the difficulties with which we have to contend and of the limitations which afflict us. It at once shows us that in the midst of apparent injustice there is, in the long run, really nothing but perfect justice for everybody; that all good fortune has been earned; that all bad fortune is deserved, and that each of us is, mentally and morally, what he has made himself. Masefield put it well when he wrote:

> All that I rightly think or do,
> Or make or spoil or bless or blast,
> Is curse or blessing justly due
> For sloth or effort in the past.
> My life's a statement of the sum
> Of vice indulged or overcome.
> And as I journey on the roads
> I shall be helped and healed and blest.
> Dear words shall cheer, and be as goads
> To urge to heights as yet unguessed.
> My road shall be the road I made.
> All that I gave shall be repaid.

Have we ever heard of a plan more just, of a truth more inspiring? It is surely a satisfying thought that every mental effort shall give increased power of intellect; that all kindly thought of others becomes a shield for our own protection in time of need; that every impulse of affection shall ripen into the love of comrades; that all lofty thinking builds heroic character, with which we shall return, in some future time, to play a still nobler part in the world of mankind.

## CHAPTER XV.

## SUPERPHYSICAL EVOLUTION

If we accept the idea of evolution at all we cannot escape the conclusion that there is superphysical evolution. The belief that man is the highest intelligence in the universe, except God Himself, is utterly inconsistent with evolutionary facts and principles. Evolution is a continuous unfolding from within, and it is only the limitation of our senses that leads us to set limitations to it. The one great life of the universe expresses itself in myriad forms and at innumerable levels of development. One of those levels is humanity. As certainly as our consciousness has evolved to its present stage it shall go on to higher ones.

The thought of Occidental civilization has been sadly fettered with materialism. It has scarcely dared to think beyond that which could be grasped with the hands. The physical senses marked out its field of investigation. What could not be seen or heard or felt had for it no existence. Modern science explored the material universe and perfected its methods until the vast panorama of worlds could be intimately studied, and its illimitable scope and colossal grandeur be somewhat comprehended; but there was no study of *life* comparable to that vast panorama of material worlds, for scientists had made the remarkable blunder of assuming that the last word on the nature of matter had been spoken. Then came the startling discoveries that revolutionized the accepted views of matter, that proved that the supposedly indivisible atom was a miniature universe, a tiny cosmos of force. The old theories about matter had to be discarded. They were as much out of date as the belief that the earth is flat; and now modern science is turning tardy attention to a study of the life side of the universe. The moment that is done the sense of consistency and the law of correspondence compel us to postulate a gradation of intelligences rising above man as man rises above the insects.

While at our stage of evolution we can no more comprehend the more highly evolved life and intelligence above and beyond us than a domestic animal can comprehend the comparatively complex life we live, we can, nevertheless, see that our environment is admirably designed to furnish the experience necessary for our mental and moral evolution and that the race as a whole is making steady progress in the development of altruistic qualities. Here is a fact of tremendous significance: the development of unselfishness in the midst of a world where, if things were controlled by physical laws alone, we should expect the opposite result; for the physical laws that guarantee the survival of the fittest give life and success and supremacy to selfish and brutal physical and mental power.

No student of nature denies the fact of evolution, denies that we are moving forward and upward in a systematic, orderly way. Now, if our evolution is ruled by chance, if we are but the product of chemical affinities and mechanical laws, as the materialists believe, then it is clear that our development should be following the course of chance; that the race would be as likely to become extinct as to achieve great progress, and that vice, ignorance, and selfishness would be quite as likely to be our ideals as purity, wisdom and benevolence.

Leaving the materialist aside and assuming, as all the rest of us are doubtless willing to do, that the universe exists for the sake of the evolution of life and is designed to develop its inherent qualities, we would expect to find, as we do, law and order everywhere from the smallest life the miscroscope reveals to the farthest reach of the telescope. Nothing would be allowed to drift. Skillful control would be found everywhere. Evolution would be supervised and directed, unfavorable conditions would be minimized and the race would be guarded and guided to the extent that was consistent with free will, and its development.

Is it not clear that something is required in evolution besides the thing to be evolved and its environment? Take, for example, children in a school. We have the children, the building and the books, but something else is required before they will make any progress. There must be a superintending intelligence that we call the teacher, and we know well enough that without that there will be chaos instead of progress.

Whoever accepts the idea of evolution at all sees

that there must be, somewhere in the universe, the higher products of evolution. We can see an orderly gradation of life running through the kingdoms below us. We observe the higher animals, and the lower, the reptiles, the insects, making an orderly decline down to the animalcule. It would be downright nonsense to suppose that evolution stops suddenly with man and that this orderly gradation there disappears; that there is no connecting chain of life between man and God, and that in this vast universe, in which our earth is like a grain of sand upon a mountain range, there is no higher product of evolution than man. That would be as irrational as some of the misconceptions of ancient days.

There was a time when our remote ancestors, huddled in an insignificant portion of the earth and constituting a very small fraction of its population, firmly believed that the earth was the center of the universe; that the sun was a small but convenient affair that existed only for the purpose of furnishing them light and that everything was arranged for the particular convenience of the people of that locality. Their conception of God was equally grotesque. They thought of Him as the ruler in the little universe their imaginations had outlined. They believed Him to be their especial protector and defender against all other peoples. We can hardly say which is the greater, the ignorance that held that conception of the universe or the vanity that led to the belief that they were the only living things worthy of consideration. We have advanced in knowledge, but how is it with vanity when we still believe that the human race is the supreme thing in evolution and, as many do, that the rest of creation, including the animals, exists only for the use of man?

As a matter of occult fact there are other lines of evolution besides the human going forward upon this particular planet, and one of these, the deva evolution, is as much higher than we, as we are higher than the animals. It is so much higher that its lowest forms are composed of etheric matter and it is not, therefore, visible to the physical senses.

However strange and improbable such a fact may seem to those who have not investigated the matter, scientific men see that it is reasonable and natural. Huxley, in "Some Controverted Questions," says that the working of consciousness in the higher cannot be understood by the lower and that there is nothing against the analogies of nature in supposing there are grades of intelligences as high above men as men are above insects!

Writing on the subject of energy, Nicola Tesla says:

"We can conceive of organized beings living without nourishment and deriving all the energy they need for the performance of their life functions from the ambient medium. * * * There may be * * * individualized material systems of beings, perhaps of gaseous constitution, or composed of substance still more tenuous. In view of this possibility—nay, probability—we cannot apodictically deny the existence of organized beings on a planet merely because the conditions on the same are unsuitable for the existence of life as we conceive it. We cannot even, with positive assurance, assert that some of them might not be present here in this our world, in the very midst of us, for their constitution and life manifestation may be such that we are unable to perceive them."*

Alfred Russell Wallace, who was called "the grand old man of science," wrote:

"I think we have got to recognize that between man and the ultimate God there is an almost infinite multitude of beings working in the universe at large, at tasks as definite and important as any we have to perform on earth. I imagine that the universe is peopled with spirits—that is, with intelligent beings—with power and duties akin to our own, but vaster. I think there is a gradual ascent from man upward and onward."

While such scientists, lacking conclusive evidence, go only to the point of asserting that it is reasonable and probable that supermen exist, the occultist asserts it as a fact within his personal knowledge.†

When we reflect upon the very narrow range of the physical senses, when we remember that it is only by receiving vibrations through the sense organs that we can be conscious of what exists about us and that with the physical organism we can receive only a small fraction of known vibrations, we ought to easily abandon the notion that because we are unconscious of a thing that is evidence against its reality.

---

* "The Conservation of Energy," Nicola Tesla, *Century Magazine*.

† *The Masters and the Path.*—C. W. Leadbeater.

To suppose that the vast cosmos exists to produce a single line of evolution, and that the frail and imperfect human being is its supreme product is absurd—an idea as provincial as the belief of our remote ancestors that the earth was the fixed center of the solar system. If there is one thing more striking than another in the phenomena that surrounds us it is that a fundamental characteristic of nature is diversity and profusion. No matter whether we turn to the animal or the vegetable kingdom we find a bewildering variety of life and the greatest complexity of production. Everywhere the universal life is seeking expression through a multiplicity of forms, and is manifesting itself in a gradation of consciousness that begins far below the point where the eye can see it and extends upwards in orderly sequence far beyond where we can see it or comprehend it.

Either life is not eternal progress and evolution is not a fact at all, or else there is a gradation of intelligences corresponding in its scope to the material universe. As the animal's comprehension is to its small world, and as our own intelligence is to our larger world, so the wisdom of higher intelligences must be to their still wider environment.

This not only commends itself to one's reason as the natural state of affairs, it not only has the endorsement of the scientific mind as the probable state of affairs, but it has been ascertained by occult investigation to be the actual state of affairs. Quite aside from the other lines of evolution going forward on the earth, the human race itself has, as one would naturally suppose it must have, its evolutionary products above us as well as below us. Towering above and beyond us, as the solar system stretches beyond the earth, are the beings of super-intelligence whose mundane evolution was completed before ours was begun. Is it not reasonable that in the hands of some of these, and lesser intelligences, must rest the great work of guiding and directing the present human evolution? From these Elder Brothers of the race come the great religions of the world and in the scriptures of every one of them will be found more or less of a description of some of these beings of the higher evolution, called by various names in the various sacred books and known in the Bible as angels and archangels. But the workaday world is so completely absorbed in material affairs, and the facts are so obscured by mysticism and poetry, that even Christians have generally come to think of this spiritual hierarchy as something very vague and far away, and as having little or nothing to do with human affairs.

Leaving all mysticism entirely aside for the moment and looking at the question with the calculating eye of science it is easy to see that evolution must have its products in the way of greater intelligences than our own, and that these intelligences must have their work in the activities of the universe as well as we ourselves. What would naturally be the work of those who are beyond us, who differ from us partly in a vastly superior intelligence, and a stronger and steadier benevolence, and who for the time being may, or may not, be living in a physical body? We may get a hint by observing what is the chosen work of those a lesser degree ahead of us in evolution, but who still live among us—the work of our greatest living souls, our thinkers, poets, philosophers, scientists? They are all teachers and leaders in human evolution—teachers and leaders of others not quite so far along.

So it must be for those higher than our humanity. In a somewhat different way they are still the teachers, the inspirers, the directors, in human evolution. Rank after rank, rising from plane to plane, this gradation of intelligences, growing more and more spiritual, ascends to the supreme heights we can not, as yet, comprehend. From these lofty heights come the spiritual impulses that guide the race, so far as the race can be guided without interference with its developing will power. It is only by an orderly gradation that such impulses can reach our groping humanity. It is very much like a great army in motion. There may be a number of directions in which it can move, some much more desirable than others. An order is issued by the staff of commanders; from them it reaches the brigadier generals; it passes on to the regimental officers; and so it travels on downward to the captains, the corporals, until it is a part of the knowledge of the entire army. In our evolution, it is not orders that are issued to be obeyed. That would destroy that priceless thing we call free will. It is rather ideals that are issued, ideals a little higher than the present accomplishment, but which our inherent divinity urges us forward to attain. This is the hidden side of evolution that the race feels, but does not see, and the occult results of which are everywhere apparent in the history of human affairs.

The point of contact for a spiritual impulse may be a single individual as it was in giving the Christian religion to the world, and as it was when John Brown became an instrument to arouse a nation from its callous toleration of human slavery and the paralysis of conscience that was growing out of it; but in this, as in all other things, there is the gradation from the most spectacular and dramatic to the most inconspicuous. Every human being who is striving to live unselfishly is a point of contact for the divine impulse that forever seeks its way into the visible human life.

Guiding the evolution of humanity is no mysterious or fantastic thing. It is merely a question of setting people thinking along the right line, of getting the necessary ideal before them, of finding one or many points of contact between the higher wisdom and the lower intelligence, and this may come through the self sacrifice of a single John Brown or through the quickened consciences of many.

Among the fairly thoughtful criticisms from the materialist's point of view is a book setting forth the declaration that nature is unintelligent because wasteful. Looking at the so-called waste that occurs in the prolific production of nature, while only a part of that production appears to fulfil its intended purpose, the author says it is as though a potter should produce pots on a large scale in order that ninety per cent could be broken and still leave the required number. That, of course, would show lack of intelligence; but is it not clear that before we can determine the wisdom, or lack of it, that characterizes any process, we must first know the full purpose of that process? If a potter is producing pots to sell and the final purpose of the production is to get as many pots as possible from a given quantity of clay, and the whole matter ends there, then destroying ninety while making a hundred would be a senseless performance; but let us suppose that instead of the prosaic business of producing pots the purpose is a wholly different one; that it is, in the first place, the training of the intelligence at work in the production and, in the second place, the evolution of the material of which pots are made to the point where it becomes possible for that material to be made into translucent vases—a point in its evolution that shall be reached simultaneously with the development of the potter's art to the level where it is equal to the making of such vases. Then there has been no waste at any time, for the purpose of the work was triple: the making of some pots of the inferior quality, the evolution of the clay to a higher quality and the evolution of the intelligence working in the clay to a higher level. There was only the appearance of waste, because the full purpose was not understood.

Looking at the apparent loss through disease and violence the critic declares that the waste presents a stupefying scene. Of course it does unless we keep in mind the stupendousness of even our little corner of the universe and have some understanding of the plan and purpose in hand. If we have no thought of a coherent whole, no idea of the object toward which nature is working, as a matter of course it will appear wasteful and unintelligent. If a very small child were to go where some vast cathedral is under construction, and but half finished, he might be barely able to make his way through the wilderness of odds and ends, of bits of stained glass and small pieces of onyx and bronze. This would appear to him like downright waste, this reckless throwing away of beautiful playthings. If he thought at all on the subject he would probably conclude that the architect was a very foolish person.

Another point put forward by our critic is that no beneficent power can be directing evolution, for nature, he asserts, is merciless because destructive. He sees this destruction going on everywhere and particularly in the animal kingdom. He seems to look upon physical life as the most desirable thing in the universe, and therefore when living things are deprived of it he calls nature merciless; but considered as a problem of evolution the form is as nothing to the progress of that life. It only drops a form in order that it may express itself in a better one. Who shall say at what particular point of the physical life it is most advantageous to do that? How do we know that death is not a blessing instead of a misfortune? If nature is really indifferent why is death practically painless? How does it happen that "merciless, senseless nature," so arranges things that the mouse or bird caught by the cat is at once stupefied? And this holds good higher up. Dr. David Livingstone, in his book on African exploration tells us that when the lion pounced upon him in the jungle and crushed his arm he felt no pain and had not even any mental distress although death seemed certain. He said that it was as though an anaesthetic had been given to him. Physicians declare that in spite of appearances to the contrary death is a physically painless process. It is only the mind that tortures, sometimes. It is not death itself, but the fear of death, or the accident or disease that leads to death, that gives pain. The assertion that nature is merciless is not consistent with these facts.

If we once start with a false premise we can afterwards reason logically and yet always go astray in the end, and this is just the mistake we make when we assume that physical life is the thing of supremest value in the universe. Another error is to regard man, because he represents the highest development of that life which we see, as the most important thing in the universe and then proceed to make his desires the standard by which to determine the wisdom and consistency of nature. It is common to say that in the bee providence has been kind or nature has been wise, while the vexatious ant is looked upon as an inscrutable blunder. This view arises simply from the fact that we are judging the wisdom of nature by the utility to man. The bee makes honey. The ant does nothing for us and often annoys us; but why should we assume that the life of the bee has no other purpose than to help feed the human race? Would not a little more thinking on the subject lead us to see that the bee is a manifestation of life that is doing a work in the universe the importance of which is in nowise dependent upon the fact that we contrive to make it give part of its time to us? Is it not quite conceivable that the marvelous little civilization of the bee would go forward just the same if there were not a human being on the earth? Only our vanity blinds us to the fact that both bees and ants are carrying forward a work in evolution as important to the universe, in its way, as our own. Darwin has shown that earth worms play a most important role in relation to the soil. Human life, its welfare and even its continued existence, is closely interwoven with all animate creation. We could not be what we are, expressing the intelligence we now possess but for the evolution of matter that has gone before through work in which we had no part. To the universe as a whole and the intelligence which plans and guides it there is surely neither the great nor the small. Each and all are equally necessary to the whole. To a clock the weights that give the driving force are of no more importance than the pendulum, nor are both of them of more consequence in achieving the purpose back of the whole mechanism than the smallest cogwheel in it.

That nature is destructive does not in the least indicate that profound wisdom is not in directive control of natural law. There is verity in that old saying, "There is no great loss without some small gain." It is true; and the reverse is equally true. There can be no great gain without some loss. We are in a world of action and reaction, and in the very nature of things neither creation nor destruction can stand entirely by itself. We have only to look about us to see that no creative work by man can possibly go forward without a certain margin of destruction. No great canal has ever been made without costing thousands of lives. Not even a great bridge is built without loss of life. No imaginable kind of achievement can be wholly free from reactionary loss. This must inevitably be so and is as true of the greater as of the lesser, as true of gods as of men. Law applies as much to the greatest intelligence as to the human. If so, then it must be that there is a constant choosing of the lesser of necessary evils. Sometimes one who is apparently the greatest destroyer is actually the most merciful. There is a story about a great general that illustrates this fact. During a battle he sent an order to a subordinate officer to move his men to a certain position. This officer failed to perceive that the general really understood what he was doing and sent him a note: "If I understand your order it means the annihilation of my command." Beneath that note the general wrote two words, "You understand," and sent it back. Of course the general knew that he was choosing the lesser of two evils and he did not hesitate to order a few hundred men to march to certain death in order to prevent the loss of ten thousand in a prolonged battle. If these soldiers were judging everything from the viewpoint of their personal interest they would certainly think it most brutal indifference to the sacredness of life. No doubt their wives and children, who knew still less of the great plan in the mind of the general, which doubtless included not merely this particular battle but looked forward to issues involving hundreds of thousands of lives, would regard the order that sent these men to death as one of the most inhuman atrocities, and possible only to a fiend incarnate.

Those who try to interpret the purpose of life without the help of a hypothesis that takes a comprehensive view of the universe are likely to go astray in their conclusions, and what is the soundest wisdom and the highest altruism may be mistaken for foolishness and cruelty. But when we set to work with the theory that the universe exists for the purpose of evolving all life, the difficulties vanish. Chaos and confusion give way to order and to law. We see a vast universe in which diversity and profusion are the natural order. We see the upward climb of all life expressed in a multiplicity of forms and showing many lines of evolution. We see an orderly gradation of intelligence below us and see the reasonableness of the idea that it must also rise above us. We see that the higher products of this evolution must, like ourselves, have their activities in consciousness. We see that their natural and reasonable relationship to us is that of teachers and leaders, of supervisors of evolution. We see in such religions as Christianity, Buddhism, Hinduism and Mohammedanism, their guiding hand at work. We see in earnest, selfless and heroic men and women the channels through which divine ideals reach our physical life. We see that the idea that nature makes mistakes has its origin in treating a fragment as though it were the whole. We see that the notion that nature is cruel arises from a misconception of the facts. We see that wisdom and beneficence are as certainly integral parts of the universe as they are growing attributes in human life.

This hypothesis is as full of reason as it is of hope. With this hypothesis the Theosophist turns his back to the materialistic night, built of the fantastic shadows of doubt, terrified by no specter of death and afflicted with no pessimism of despair.

While the relationship of the supermen to the human race is that of teachers, guardians and directors, that relationship is not at all that which is expressed in the term "spirit guides," so frequently used by spiritualists. That is a totally different thing. They seem to imply that the "spirit guide" gives direct instructions or orders to the person known as a "medium." Evolution can proceed only if we use our initiative in the affairs of life. If we were to be directed by the wisdom and will of others we would not evolve at all. We would be merely automata animated by others, and no matter how great they were we could never develop our judgment and self-reliance. It is not thus that the great spiritual hierarchy guides human evolution. It is, in part, by working with mankind en masse and bringing mental and moral forces to play upon them, thus stimulating latent intellectual and spiritual forces from within. In another direction it is actual superintendence, or administration, or teaching, in a way that does not interfere with one's initiative or will. If the soul is to evolve it must have liberty—even the freedom to make mistakes.

It is sometimes asked why, if the supermen exist, those who are in incarnation do not come out into the world and give us ocular evidence of the fact. It is pointed out that they could speedily convince the world by a display of superphysical force; but they are probably not in the least interested in convincing anybody of their existence. They *are* interested in raising the general level of morality, of course, but such an exhibition would not make people morally better. The work of the supermen can best be done from higher planes than the physical. As for the very small number of the supermen who take physical bodies the better to do their special work, they can best accomplish it from secluded places; and if they sometimes have reason to come out into the seething vibrations of our modern civilization it is easy to understand that they would not, to the ordinary observer, be conspicuously different from other men.

Perhaps the most important of the various reasons why They do not live more among human beings is that such a course would be an enormous loss of energy. Their work is done chiefly from the mental and still higher planes where a given amount of energy will accomplish thousands of times more than it would on the physical plane.

It is from the Spiritual Hierarchy that all the religions of the world come. There the question may arise, "Then why do they differ so greatly?" Because the peoples to whom they are given differ. The difference of temperament and viewpoint between the Orient and the Occident is enormous. We are evolving along the outer, the objective, and our civilization represents the material conquest of nature. They are evolving different faculties. In the Orient the common trend of conversation is philosophical, just as in the Occident it is commercial. Such different types of mind require somewhat different statements of ethics, but the fundamental principles of all religions are identical.

As individuals differ so do races. Let us imagine that the world had never had any ethical teaching and one man had thought out a moral code of his own. He begins teaching it. The first man he meets is obviously a high type. He says to him, "My friend, here is something which I have worked out that may help you. It is this—do to others as you would have them do to you." Now, simply because this person has much inner refinement, he would reply, "That's magnificent! I have never thought of human relationships in just those terms; but, of course, if we all practiced your precept it would establish a heaven on earth. I shall try to live up to your lofty ideal."

Pleased with his success he goes on to the next man and presents the same idea. But this man is far down in the evolutionary scale. He has never thought of the welfare of anybody but himself. He is still engaged in the sharp practices of the world. He cheats his neighbor whenever he gets the opportunity. This man is amazed by such teaching. He finds it difficult to believe it sane. Realizing, then, that such a moral code is too high for him the teacher brings the ideal down to his comprehension by saying, "How will this do—do to others as they do to you?"

"Why, that's common sense," he replies. "I don't always do it but I really think I should. We should all give to others as good treatment as they give us. I'm willing to try to live up to that; but your other proposition, that we should treat others as we would like to be treated regardless of what they do to us is simply foolish."

The first man readily took the highest statement of ethics because he was far enough along in evolution to appreciate its beauty. The second man rejected it because it was too advanced for his mental and moral grasp. Had the teacher insisted upon giving him what the other man readily took he would have lost him altogether.

The difference between men in the street is no greater than the difference between the various peoples of the earth. A spiritual truth put in one way is effective with one people but does not move another. While religions are essentially the same in principle their presentation must differ as peoples differ, each religion giving to those to whom it is presented what is best suited to serve the evolutionary need of that era.

When a new era in human evolution begins, a World Teacher comes into voluntary incarnation and founds a religion that is suited to the requirements of the new age. Humanity is never left to grope along alone. All that it can comprehend and utilize is taught it in the various religions. World Teachers, the Christs and saviours of the race, have been appearing at propitious times since humanity began existence.

Most readers will probably agree that a World Teacher known as the Christ did come and that He founded a religion nearly two thousand years ago. Why do they think so? They reply that God so loved the world that He sent His Son, the Christ, to bring it light and life. If that is true how can we avoid the conclusion that He, or His predecessors, must have come many a time before? The belief that He came but once is consistent only with the erroneous notion that Genesis is history instead of allegory, and that the earth is about six thousand years old! Science has not determined its age but we know that it is very old, indeed. Many eminent scientists have made rough estimates, taking into consideration all that we have learned from such sources as astronomy, geology and archeology.

It is interesting to observe that the estimated age of the earth grows with our knowledge of nature. Many years ago such scientists as Joly and Bosler, basing their calculations on the time necessary to produce the sodium content of the ocean and upon the radio activity of the rocks, made estimates varying from one hundred million to seven hundred million years, but today the scientist talks of the age of the earth in thousands of millions of years.*

In the face of such facts what becomes of the assertion that God so loved the world that He sent

---

* The estimate by scientists of two thousand million years is in substantial agreement with theosophical teaching.

His Son to help ignorant humanity about two thousand years ago—but never before? What about the hundreds of millions of human beings who lived and died before that time? Did He care nothing for them? Did He give his attention to humanity for a period of only two thousand years and neglect it for millions of years? Does anybody believe that God, in His great compassion, sent just one World Teacher for that brief period? What would we say of a father who gave one hour of his whole life to his child and neglected him absolutely before and after that? Countless millions of the people who lived and died prior to the coming of the Christ were very much like ourselves. They belonged to ancient civilizations that often surpassed our own in many desirable characteristics. They were educated and cultured in their time and fashion. They were fathers and sons and mothers and daughters and husbands and wives, with the same kind of heart ties that we have. What of them? Were they permitted to grope in the moral wilderness without a Teacher or a ray of light? Of course the idea is preposterous. If God so loved the world that He sent His Son two thousand years ago He sent Him, or some predecessor, very many times before.

The Supermen are not myths nor figments of the imagination. They are as natural and comprehensible as human beings. In the regular order of evolution we shall ourselves reach their level and join their ranks while younger humanities shall attain our present state. As they arose we, too, shall rise. Our past has been evolution's night. Our present is its dawn. Our future shall be its perfect day. Think of that night from which we have emerged — a chaos of contending forces, a world in which might was the measure of right, a civilization of scepter and sword, of baron and serf, of master and slave. That, we have left behind us. We have reached the grey dawn of a real civilization, of a public conscience, of individual liberty, of collective welfare, of the sacredness of life, but with armed force still dominant, with war still the arbiter of national destiny, with conflict between the higher aspirations and the lower desires still raging—a world of refined brutality, of selfishness masked by custom, of cruelty disguised by usage. In all that we now live. But think of the age that is coming —an era in which love shall replace force, a time when sabre and cannon shall be unknown, when selfish desires shall be transmuted into noble service, when we who now live on the earth shall finish human evolution and join the Spiritual Hierarchy to direct the faltering steps of a younger humanity. That is the magnificent future the Theosophist sees for the human race.

# INDEX

Ancestors ............................................244
Animal instincts ................................... 20
Aphasia ............................................ 80
Astral body ........................................ 89
    a duplicate of physical body .................... 69
    its rearrangement ............................. 87
Automatic writing ................................. 39
Astral world or region ............................. 79
    different types ................................101
    food, clothing, shelter ......................81, 96
    freedom in ..................................... 97
    length of stay there .....................83, 84, 102
    not vague ...................................... 81
    not punitive ................................... 82
    service on ..................................... 99
    shortest life a prize ...........................100
    subdivisions of ................................ 83
    the savage ....................................103
    varieties of work on .......................... 98

Bees and ants .....................................254
Bodies ............................................ 60
    are vehicles of consciousness ................... 64
    creation of ................................ 62, 63
    constantly changing ........................... 67
    mental and spiritual .......................... 61
    new ones a necessity ..........................142
    not the man ................................... 68
Boy murderer .................................148, 149
Brain, a limitation of memory .....................189

Causal body ..............................122, 123, 199
Cause and effect, the law of ......................210
    evidence of ..............................211, 212
    why such law .................................217
Child is old soul in new body .....................228
Clairvoyance .................................. 44, 45
    two types of ................................... 47

```
Collective consciousness, The .......................137
Conflict between higher and lower .................227
Consciousness and matter ........................... 14
Creation ........................................... 32
    not yet finished ...........................180, 181
Cremation .........................................111
Cross correspondence ............................... 38
Crookes' experimenta ............................... 34

Dead, The, our thought of them ............108, 109, 110
Death, a release ................................... 50
    a beneficent destroyer ......................... 73
    affects only the physical body ................. 72
    delusions about ............................ 76, 77
    fear of ........................................ 71
    is painless .................................... 73
    its evolutionary value ..................... 74, 75
    it does not change man ......................... 77
    three modes of ................................. 87
Deformity .............................. 91, 92, 93, 238
Destruction, by nature ............................247
    may be beneficent .............................255

Ego and personality ...........................197, 198
Elder brothers of race ........................248, 249
Emanation .......................................... 19
Emerson, teaching of ........................... 24, 25
    quoted ......................................... 68
Emotions .................................. 95, 96, 104
    control of ............................108, 109, 110
    registered in matter ..........................237
Eternal possessions ...............................205
Etheric double ..................................... 65
Evolutionary progress .............................137
Forces determine destiny ..........................220
Fools and idiots ..................................178
Free will .....................................222, 249

Group soul ........................................140
Guiding evolution .................................250

Hell, threat of ...................................141
    self created ..................................150
Heredity ..........................................155
    mental and emotional .........................156
```

Horse in evolution .................................170

Idiocy .........................................150, 238
Immanence .......................... 13, 17, 18, 23, 24
Intellect and morality ..............................179
Irregularity of development ........................ 180

Judgement Day ....................................219
"Judge not" ......................................232

Lodge, Sir Oliver ............................... 35, 36
Lodge and Haeckel ................................114
Luck .............................................233

"Memory of nature" ..............................230
Memory of past lives ..........................185, 187
    why we should not remember .................192
Materialism ........................... 15, 16, 22, 166
Materialization .................................... 35
Masefield quoted ..................................239
Matter, grades of .................................. 60
Mediums, definition of .......................... 36, 37
Mechanical view of creation .......................177
Mental plane .................................. 84, 86
Saul and Samuel ..................................105
Natural law, its immutability ......................216

Occult scientists ............................... 47, 49
Opportunity, loss of, reward for ....................213
Origin of race .....................................165
Other evolutions ..................................245

Pain .............................................225
Personality, survival of ......................... 40, 42
    is fragment ..................................196
Planes, defined ................................... 51
    the mental plane ............................. 55
    their sub-division ............................. 57
Preexistence ......................................168
Premonitions .................................... 20
Progress of race .............................172, 173
Psychic phenomena ..............................106
Psychic science ................................... 33
Purgatory ..................................... 88, 91
Purpose of life ...................................256

Race evolution .......................................171
Reactions ............................................231
Reaping and sowing ..............................219
Reincarnation .......................................113
    an opportunity ..................................161
    explains ........................................149
    its utility ......................................201
    and instinct ...................................140
    and justice ....................................145
    promotes morality .............................205
    no element of chance in ...................157, 159
    poems on ......................................162
    what soul gains from .........................190
Religions of the world ............................258
Responsibility a moral foundation ..............202, 204

Salvation ............................................169
Scientific basis of morality ......................... 27
Schurz, Carl, experience of ..................... 42, 43
Sex, in evolution ...................................174
Shaping our future ................................236
Skill not dependent on memory ....................192
Skill and wisdom .................................141
Sleep ............................................ 69, 124
Space ............................................... 56
Soul, likened to actor .............................182
    between incarnations .........................119
    compared to naturalist ........................120
    defined .........................................120
    and new body .................................115
    partial expression of ..........................117
    its material mechanism ....................... 122
    its permanent home ..........................118
    its preexistence ...............................118
Souls of a kind are drawn together .................224
Special creation ...............................146, 152
    does not explain ..............................153
"Spirit guides" ....................................257
Supermen, not myths ............................262
    work of ........................................258
Superphysical evolution ..........................241
Suicide ............................................. 88

Theosophy, both old and new ........................ 8
   meaning of the word ........................... 9
   not transplanted ............................... 9
   not a religion .................................. 10
   and theology ................................... 10
Tesla's thought ...................................... 245
Testimony of Dr. Livingstone ........................ 252
Thoughts and desires are forces ..................... 213
Thought forms ....................................... 215
Typist illustration .................................. 191

Ultimate atom ...................................... 54
Unity of life .................................... 25, 26

Wallace, Alfred Russell, quoted .................... 246
Waste, is apparent loss ....................... 251, 252
Why religions differ .......................... 258, 260
Wilcox, Ella Wheeler ............................... 235
World growing better .............................. 136